FURNITURE UPHOLSTERY AND REPAIR

By James B. Johnstone
and the Sunset Editorial Staff

LANE PUBLISHING CO. • MENLO PARK, CALIFORNIA

Foreword

The art of furniture upholstery is well suited to the home craftsman. Upholstery offers a wide range of do-it-yourself projects, from building an entirely new piece of furniture to repairing or restyling an old one. A beginning upholsterer can achieve good results with less experience and manual skill than are needed for many other crafts. It takes patience—each procedure must be checked carefully before you proceed to the next—but the rewards are many.

This book takes you step by step through the stages of upholstering a piece of furniture. Materials and tools are described, and often alternatives are suggested for special equipment. The basic tools are a tack hammer, heavy-duty shears, sharp knives, a webbing stretcher, a ripping tool, needles, upholsterer's pins or skewers, and a mallet. The major piece of equipment required is a sewing machine—a home-type machine is adequate for much upholstery sewing; you can rent a heavy-duty machine for very heavy fabrics, have a professional upholsterer sew them, or sew them by hand. A pair of wooden trestles or sturdy table can be used to hold your project at a convenient level while you are working on it.

Quality is important in both tools and workmanship. Good tools and careful craftsmanship will be evident in the appearance of the completed piece of furniture, and your investment of time and money will be well repaid by the long-term satisfaction you will receive.

Edited by Phyllis Elving

ACKNOWLEDGEMENTS

We acknowledge with gratitude the aid of many individuals who volunteered their furniture, materials, time, and experience toward the preparation of this book. Special thanks are due to Mr. Werner A. Hauser of Jensen-Hauser Custom Upholsterers, Menlo Park, California; Bayshore Upholstery Supply & Fabric Company of San Jose, California; Garland Fabrics of San Jose, California; and Delaney Brothers Upholstery of Palo Alto, California.

Photographs by James B. Johnstone except the following:
Ells Marugg, cover and page 77.

Illustrations by Susan Lampton.

Executive Editor, Sunset Books: David E. Clark

Thirteenth Printing January 1977

 Library of Congress No. 72-115163. ISBN Title No. 0-376-01180-7. Lithographed in the U.S.A.

Contents

Special Features

Frame Building, Repair, and Restyling

The rigid frame of a piece of furniture determines its general shape and size and the style of upholstery. If you build, repair, restyle, or reinforce a frame, it will be worth the extra time and effort to use the best materials and techniques. The very finest upholstery cannot hide a frame failure.

MATERIALS AND TOOLS

To produce a good frame you must select the proper materials. First comes the important choice of wood. Then you must choose the dowels or other fasteners and the glue which are best for your project.

Woods

Woods for framing are traditionally medium-hard hardwoods with straight, close grain and no evidence of knots, especially where tacks, dowels, or other fasteners are to be used. The swirled grain around even the tightest knot prevents accurate tacking of upholstery material.

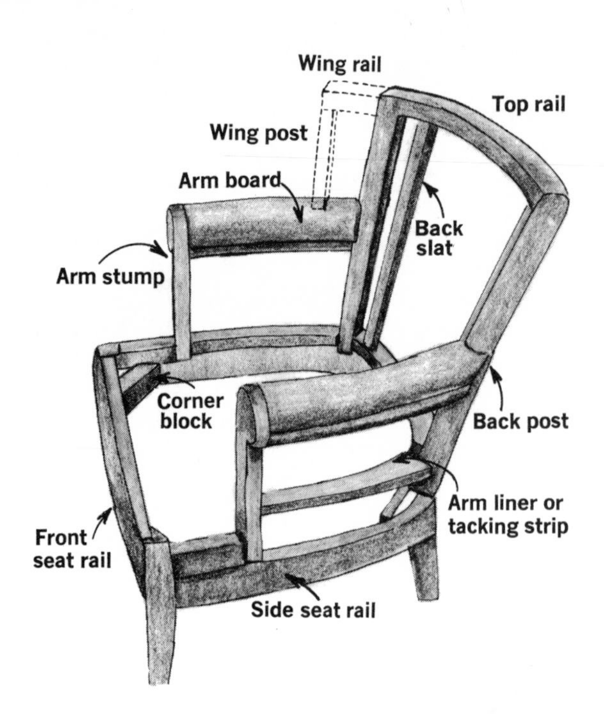

Resist the temptation to use inferior wood for a covered frame, though this practice often is used for commercially produced furniture. The extra cost for better wood is repaid many times over by ease of tacking, lack of splinters, and sturdiness of the finished piece.

Exposed and finished parts of a frame (referred to as "show wood") can be any kiln-dried, fine cabinet wood such as birch, cherry, gum, mahogany, maple, rosewood, teak, or walnut. If hard maple, rosewood, or other very hard, dense wood is used where it is necessary to drive tacks or decorative nails, be sure to predrill holes slightly smaller than the tack or nail. Otherwise you will spend hours driving the tacks or nails and removing bent ones. Worse yet, you may split the wood.

Wood used for hidden framing need not be as attractive as the portions that show, but it should be of a medium-hard, split-resistant, straight-grained hardwood such as alder, ash, birch, gum, poplar, or soft maple.

Dowels, screws, nuts, and bolts

Nails are not reliable holding devices in furniture frames and should be avoided except as temporary locating or glue-clamping devices.

Hardwood dowels used for frame joints are available in most hardware stores in 3 or 4-foot lengths and in diameters from ⅛ inch through 1 inch. They have to be cut to size and glue-grooved (see page 6) before using. Spiral dowel pins are available at many hardware and lumber outlets. They come in ¼, ⅜, and ½-inch diameters and in lengths from 1½ to 2½ inches.

A doweling jig is handy if you plan to do much frame-making, since it permits accurate hole location and ensures the correct drill-to-surface angle.

Screws are useful in frame construction for installing metal parts or bracing members or for attaching parts designed for removal—such as arms,

DOWELING JIG ensures accurate dowel hole location and angle. In foreground are replaceable drill bit guides.

STAGGER dowels wherever maximum twist resistance is required. Spirals in dowels allow excess glue to escape.

seats, wings, or decorative pieces. Glued butt joints clamped with screws are quite strong, but don't rely on them when you need the far greater strength obtainable through dowel joints.

Nuts and bolts are used for wood-to-metal joints and for some glueless, demountable wood-to-wood joints. Often the nuts are one of several wood-gripping varieties such as T-nuts. Glueless nut and bolt wood-to-wood joints can be made fairly strong, but they have a predictable habit of loosening up—especially if they are inaccessible.

Glues

Use plastic resin, aliphatic resin, casein, waterproof resorcinol, liquid hide, or hot-hide glues. The aliphatic resin and hide glues often are unavailable through local stores, but they can be obtained from mail order wood craft suppliers.

Do not use the commonly available "white glues" if continuous heavy shearing (pressure paralleling the joint) or pulling loads will be encountered. Many "white glues" have a tendency to creep and eventually fail under continued stress.

Contact cements and all other rubber-based glues are useless in load-bearing frame joints but may be useful for gluing foam, fabric, or stuffing material.

FRAME BUILDING

The choice of frame style is so dependent on personal taste that it would be impossible to give all-inclusive illustrations here. Studying one or two pieces of reupholstered furniture will probably teach you more about frame construction than looking at many pictures.

All wood should be finished on all four sides to prevent snagging of padding and covers. Round and smooth all corners around which fabric or stuffing will be pulled. Major structural parts of a frame should be at least 1¼-inch lumber. Slats and liners used to tack spring covers, muslins, and final covers should be at least 1-inch lumber.

Doweling

Of the more reliable framing joints, dowel-and-glue joints are the easiest to use. Occasionally more sophisticated mortise-and-tenon, miter, finger, tongue-and-groove, or other types of joints may be necessary for appearance on visible portions of the frame. However, don't spend time on hidden joints without first examining the decorative possibilities of exposed joints. Some designers of modern pieces go to great lengths to give the appearance of exposed joining members that are not actually used as such. Examples of such designs include the rounded dowel pegs on Early American styles; the lap, tenon, finger, and through dovetails on Scandinavian imports; and the dowel and butterfly dovetail inlays in table tops.

If either or both ends of the dowel are to show, simply clamp the two pieces together in the desired position and drill through one into the other with a drill the same size as the dowel to be used.

If hidden or blind doweling is required, predrill one piece, then use the appropriate size from a set of commercial dowel centers to locate the center of the mating hole. If a hole is located incorrectly, simply glue in a matching dowel, allow glue to dry, cut off flush, and redrill in the correct location.

The dowel diameter should never exceed half the narrowest dimension of the surface to be doweled. Two or more dowels are desirable where the piece must resist twisting forces, such as tied springs or the constant pull of low profile springs (see page 7).

Most dowel holes are drilled on the centerline of the narrower of the two pieces to be joined so that the largest possible dowel size can be used. Some workers prefer to stagger the holes and use dowels ⅛ or 3/16 inch smaller in diameter than the maximum size possible. They often move the dowels closer together and add an extra dowel for every three dowels used in the centerline method. Thus, if two ½-inch dowels spaced 3 inches apart would normally be used on the centerline in a 1-inch-wide joint, three ⅜ or 5/16-inch dowels might be used 1½ inches apart for staggered drilling. The advantage is a slight increase in dowel glue surface (the surface of the dowel which can be glued) and an increase in twist resistance.

Prepare smooth dowels for blind doweling by cutting them to a length ⅛ inch less than the depths of the two holes in the joint added together. Chamfer (taper the edges) both ends and either cut a shallow 1/16 or ⅛-inch slot in the length or use the serrated jaws of a pair of pliers to produce a long gear-toothed effect along the whole length.

Smooth dowels driven into tight-fitting glue-filled holes act as pistons producing such high pressure that the glue often forces its way out by splitting the wood. The lengthwise slots, spirals, or gear-toothing in dowels provide escape routes for excess glue and allow it to exit inside the butt joint where it can be used or removed as it is squeezed out the edges.

Where one end of the dowel is exposed, simply chamfer the leading end, slot or groove the sides, apply glue, drive in the dowel, and cut off the end flush with the surface.

Glue should be applied to both dowel and hole. In the case of plier-crimped dowels, work reasonably fast or the water in the glue will swell out the crimped surfaces flush again before they have performed their glue-escape-route function.

Glue blocks should be used whenever possible on all weight-bearing joints. Too many commercial pieces built to meet price competition lack glue

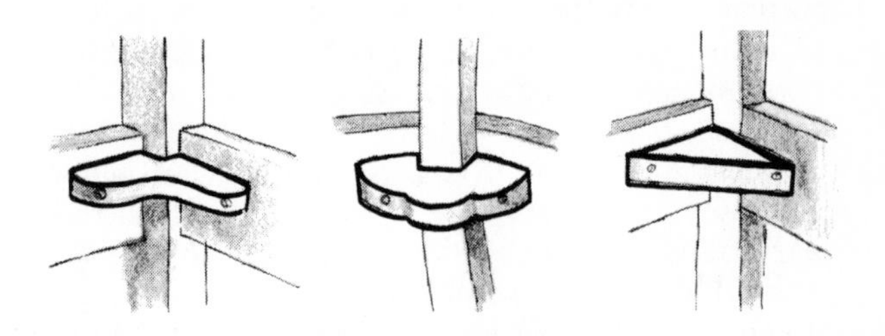

blocks, or at best have malfitting "bridge span" type blocks that meet at two slender points instead of having the maximum gluing surface obtainable with

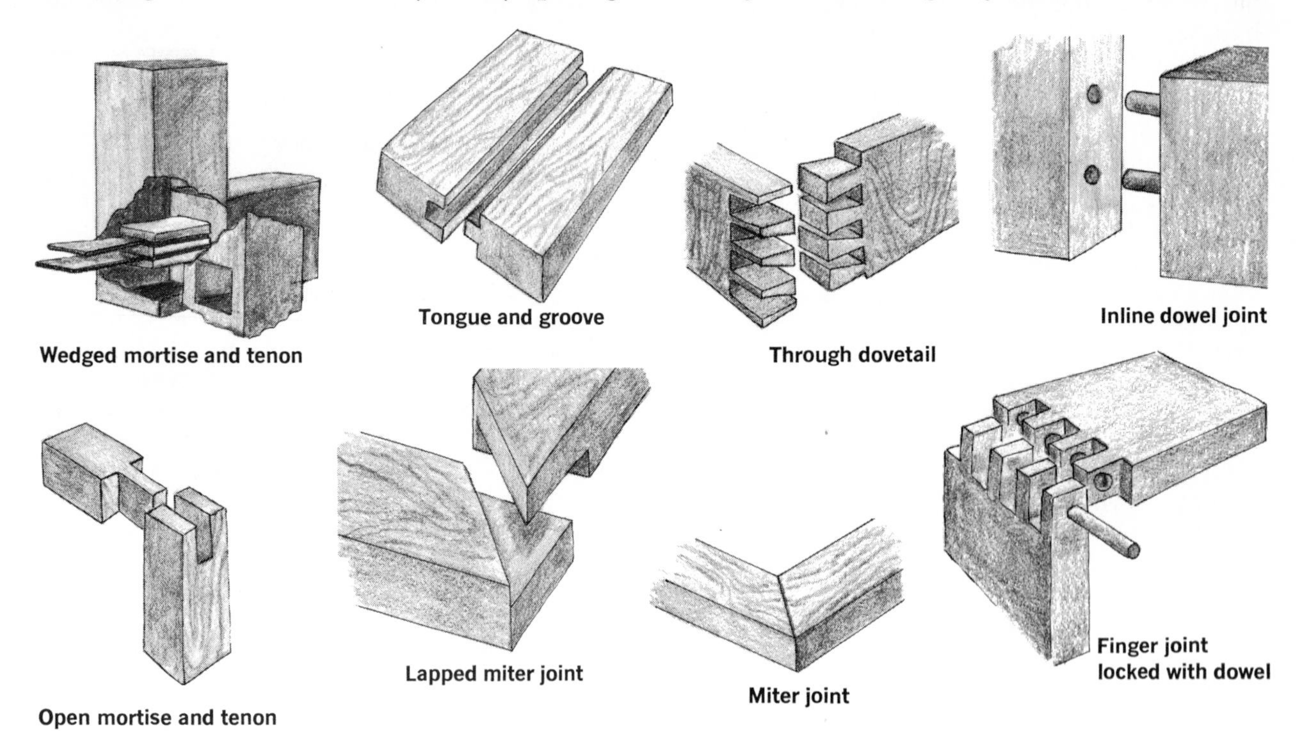

FRAMING JOINTS most commonly used are dowel (right), mortise and tenon (left). The others shown here are used most often on exposed wood sections where they are decorative as well as functional.

a fitted block. Always add blocks to the leg-to-base and base-to-back-and-arm joints of pieces you find without them if the additions can be reasonably made. It is disturbing to reupholster an apparently sturdy, blockless commercial frame and have it become wobbly a few months later, when added glue blocks could have prevented trouble.

Frames for low profile springs

Several of the low profile springs, including zig-zag, coil extension loops, rubber webbing, and some coil spring and steel strap combinations (see page 20), exert large and continuous pulling forces between the front and back seat rails, with very little pulling force between the side rails. Frames for this type of spring should be constructed with heavy front and rear seat rails to withstand the continuous pull.

All joints should have at least two dowels spaced to prevent twisting under pressure. For the strongest frame use staggered doweling.

To ensure maximum spacing block action, side rails should fit between and be overlapped by the ends of front and rear rails. Top rails should be mounted on top of the back posts, with the pull-through liner either heavily corner blocked, notched, or mortised-and-tenoned into the posts.

All frame openings over 24 inches wide must have front-to-rear braces or top-to-bottom slats. Slat-to-slat and slat-to-side rail spacing must never exceed 24 inches, though it may be less. Both a 26-inch-wide and a 48-inch-wide seat would have at least a single fore-and-aft brace, and a 72-inch couch would have at least two braces in the seat and two slats in the back. The braces and slats must be attached by dowel and glue. You may use either a swayback brace—with a 2½ to 3-inch center drop—or a flat brace mounted between the bottom edges of the front and back rails with triangular corner blocks reaching up to the top edge of the rails and out along the brace for 6 to 8 inches.

If distinct attached cushion effects are desired, double 1-inch-thick slats spaced 1 inch apart must be used for pull-through tacking slats.

Corners must be reinforced with fitted glue blocks to provide maximum gluing surface. Glue blocks should be placed so the upper surface is within 1 inch of the top spring-bearing rail surface.

Foam and airtight covers

Wherever foam or airtight covers such as natural or synthetic leathers are used, be sure to allow for escape and return of air. Foam used under porous fabric and on a solid wood base requires two ½-inch holes per square foot of wood surface. Foam or spring and pad over a solid wood base and under

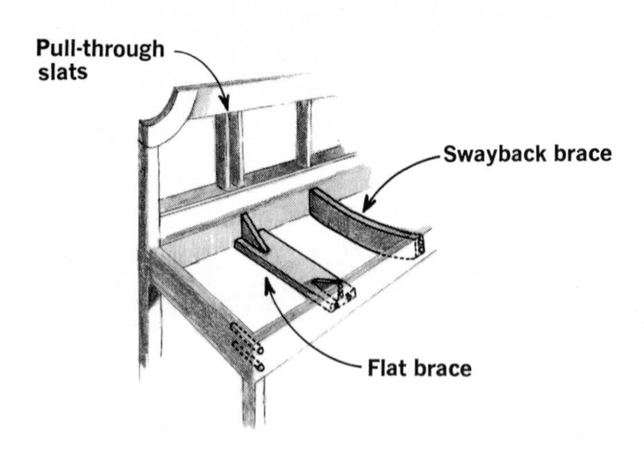

airtight vinyl covers requires four ½-inch holes per square foot of wood surface. This is the minimum venting desirable to prevent both the "whooshing" sound of escaping air when sat upon and the puckered-sack look of slow air return.

FRAME REPAIR

The most common frame repairs are regluing and reinforcing wobbly joints, repairing or replacing broken legs, backs, wings, or arms, and repairing broken or split seat or top rails.

If joint dowels and their matching holes are still tight, simply free the dowel of old glue, clean out the old glue escape channels or make new ones, then reglue and clamp.

Grossly oversized or misshapen dowel holes should be drilled out and plugged with glued wood inserts, then redrilled for new dowels.

Reinforcements can be added to most joints by means of tailored corner glue blocks.

Strengthening thin seat rails

Occasionally you will run across an exquisite heirloom-type chair with the seat rail too narrow to provide sufficient stiffness for even reasonably tight webbing, use of low profile springs, or firm leg attachment. In this case, you have three choices of handling the situation.

First, you can hand-fit and glue a second seat rail inside the old one, making sure of maximum fitted gluing surface including any leg contact points. The top edge of the rail insert may be tapered inward to prevent any major difference in feel of the resprung seat. Reweb and spring or pad as for normal upholstery.

A second choice is inserting plywood to fit the total opening. Use glue blocks to hold it in place as near to the bottom of the rail as possible. Use shorter springs when respringing, or shorten existing ones by the "run-in" method shown on page 14. Mount springs to plywood insert with tacks or staples, use a burlap or cotton "silencer" strip (page 12) and tie springs as usual (page 15).

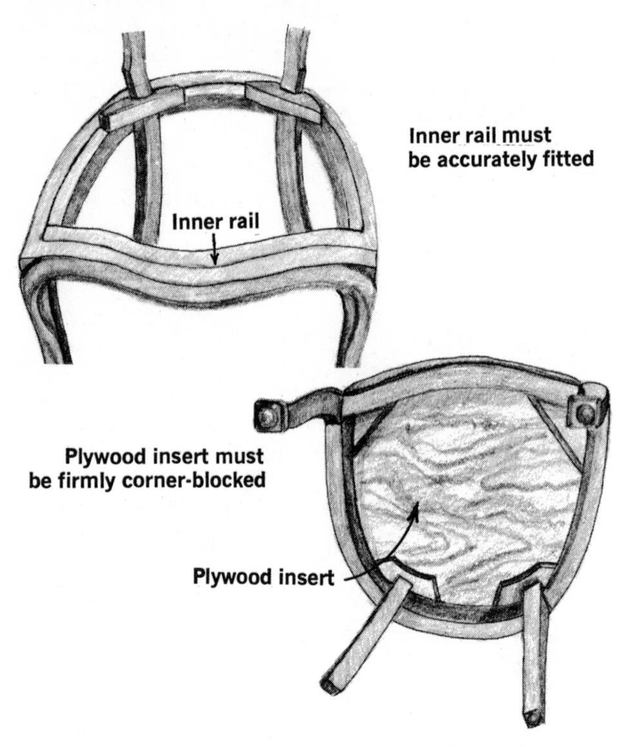

The third alternative is to use the plywood insert as described above, but move it nearer the top of the rail, and replace springs and stuffing with foam. In most cases two layers of foam are best (see page 33), the lower layer being high density and the top medium or soft density depending on the feel desired. This two-layer use prevents you from sinking down to the board. Be sure to vent the board for air passage (see page 7).

Repairing broken legs, backs, arms

Broken legs, backs, or arms are usually most easily repaired if they are green stick or with-the-grain fractures, since they tend to fit together well and provide maximum gluing surface. Simple gluing and clamping may work, but may merely repair a problem at that immediate spot only to have it recur nearby. Use a dowel glued up through the problem area. Drill up through the break—you may need an extra long drill bit, available on order from most of the bigger hardware suppliers—and glue in a properly grooved long dowel. Some of the excessively slender, more delicate type heirlooms have steel dowel rods epoxied in by experts, even though purist collectors frown on the practice.

Shattered edge, across-the-grain fractures require either replacing the specific piece or cutting away

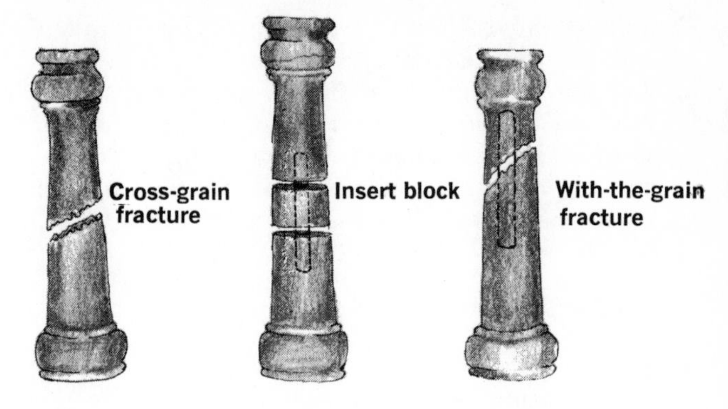

the shattered area, fitting an insert, then gluing and clamping it in place with one or more reinforcing dowels.

FRAME RESTYLING

Frame restyling is in many respects a very simple operation. The basic frame can be subtracted from or added to as long as its essential limitations are realized. It is difficult to make a gossamer Louis XIV out of a massive hide-a-bed, or a hide-a-bed out of a slab door modern. The very simplicity of frame restyling can be misleading, however, if you attack it with insufficient planning. Don't forget to allow for thickness of padding—if you want a 4-inch-wide arm, the frame will be 3 inches or less in width to allow for padding. Don't forget to allow for pull-through liners and slats—especially where single liner slats in the back are attached but separate cushion construction requires pull throughs (see sketch on page 7).

There are dozens of small things that can be done to a basic frame which will make major styling and comfort changes. Changes as small as removing all or parts of legs and substituting ball casters can make large utility and visual changes. Leg styles on short-legged overstuffed chairs or couches often can be changed simply by unscrewing legs held on by lag-bolt-and-screw-plate or T-nut, then substituting another style.

If the leg is an extension of the corner post, consider sawing it off flush with the base and fitting a new leg with dowels and glue. Hide the joint with the upholstered base (a carved line at the joint will continue the visual effect of a base line across the leg), or pigmented wiping stains.

Changing the seat construction

Seats can be changed from pad to spring construction or vice versa, or from spring or pad to foam. Pad-to-spring seat conversion requires a minimum 3-inch seat rail height. Many pad-seated chairs have less, so hardwood strips the same width as the rails must be glued to the top to achieve the 3-inch minimum. If the new strips connect to arm stumps or back posts, remove any old finish by scraping at the point of contact and fit the joint so that it will in effect act as a high quality glue block. Proceed with tying springs in place (see page 15). When complete, the legs will probably have to be shortened to compensate for increased seat height. In the case of a shaped claw or ball foot it might be wise to remove an appropriate section above the foot and repair as for a broken leg (see page 8).

Spring-to-pad seat conversion usually requires only that webbing be removed from bottom to top of frame. However, if the original seat was sprung high above the rail, it may be necessary to add height to the rails with hardwood strips so that the original seat height can be maintained.

Spring-to-foam seat conversion can be handled the same as spring-to-pad conversion, or you can fit and glue-block a piece of plywood into the seat rail opening and follow the third procedure given for repairing a weak seat rail (page 8).

Restyling arms

Arm restyling can often give the appearance of an overall style change. Narrowing, widening, raising, lowering, and shaping are the major possibilities.

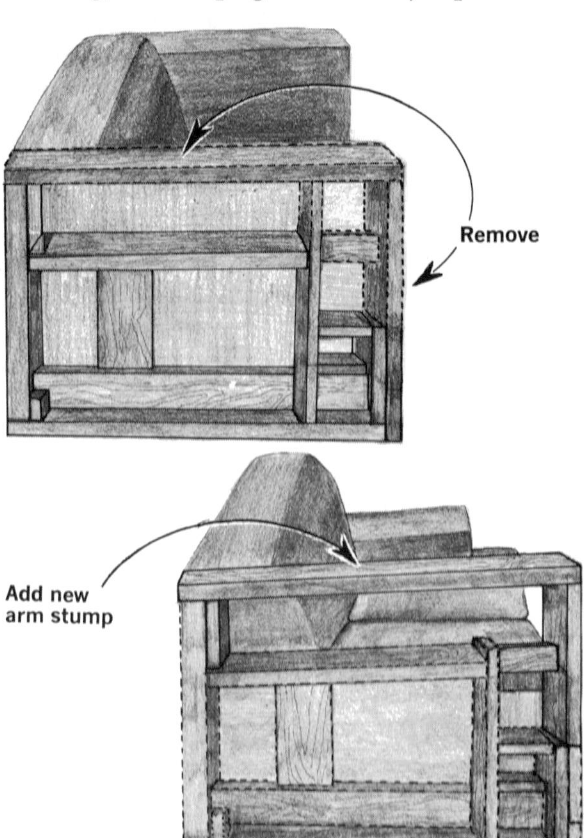

The wide sloping or boxy Lawson arms of another era can be slenderized simply by sawing off some of the width. Low arms can be raised by adding a matching superstructure, using a screw, dowel, and glue. High arms can be lowered by sawing off the excess and adding a new top board. Return arms—requiring T-cushions to lap in front of the return—can be brought forward by means of a simple F-shaped arm addition. Flush-to-the-front arms can be made into stylish return arms by cutting back the arm, installing a new arm stump 5 inches from the front rail, and adding a seat-rail filler for T-cushion support.

Arm additions to occasional and side chairs are simple if you keep the arms in the return style—front of arm set back from front of seat. Return arms can be made as self contained units and added with no other basic changes.

Flush arms—those that come all the way to the seat front—are usually handled by sawing off the existing front legs level with the seat rail, leaving the stump in the chair as a structural glue block, and making new legs as extensions of the new arm stumps. This keeps leg and arm in one smooth line.

Reshaping backs

Backs can be reshaped for both style and comfort. Hard or caned backs can be sprung or padded, partially upholstered open backs closed, or fully upholstered styles changed. Fancy scrolled toprails can be sawed off to straighten lines, wings added or removed, square tops rounded off, round top edges flattened, and flat edges rounded. Adjust the height of the pull-through liner or tack rails to match any seat height changes. When closing open backs, remove the old lower back rail after the new pull-through liner is glued in place.

Covering or adding exposed wood

Simple surface changes with large dividends can be made by covering exposed wood or adding exposed wood sections. Many a chair has been updated simply by removing carved arms and upholstering the area. The elaborately carved show wood along the bottom rim of the seat rail on some period styles may clash with adjoining furniture. The carving can be removed or simply upholstered to make the piece more compatible with its neighbors.

Conversely, a severely modern no-show-wood piece can be warmed up considerably by the addition of a show wood strip along the bottom of the seat rail, on arm fronts, or on the back top rail. Simply attach finished wood strips to the frame.

Springs and Their Supports

Many factors affect the durability, flexibility, and resiliency of springs in upholstered furniture. The size, gauge, and shape of the springs themselves all enter in, as do the method, height, and shape of tying; the quality of spring supports and their placement and anchoring; and the standard of workmanship.

Coil compression springs are the most commonly used type of spring and are available in several styles and many variations in diameter, height, and gauge. Coil extension springs are smaller and are used at the edges of folding cots and some metal furniture; they hold the metal straps that crisscross frame openings. Less familiar are the cordlike, brown, rubber-covered seat springs used in Scandinavian imports; these are really long, thin coil extension springs with rubber or plastic covers.

Non-sagging or zig-zag springs are sinuous, snake-like steel wire springs used where low profile springing is required (see page 20). Many manufacturers use them simply because they are cheaper to install than coil springs. If properly installed and upholstered, they will often outlast coil springs, but they have a noticeable difference in feel.

WEBBING OPEN FRAMES

There are basically two kinds of spring supports: the frame itself, in the case of all the low profile springs; and some form of webbing stretched across the frame opening to support coil springs or foam, which is in a sense an integrated spring and padding material. The webbing can be made of fabric, metal, or wood. Resilient rubber webbing often is used for very low profile springing to support springs or foam pillows.

Webbing seats

Good webbing that is properly spaced, stretched, and tacked to a well built frame will give years of wear even under hard use. Any reduction in quality of webbing, spacing, stretching, tacking, or frame building will reduce the expected life span.

Fabric is the traditional webbing material. Start with the best grade of jute webbing available to you; the cost difference between it and the next lower grade is negligible. Three-inch webbing is used for backs and arms, 3½ or 4-inch for seats, depending on strength desired.

Webbing tools and supplies include the webbing itself, a tack hammer, a webbing stretcher (see below), a pair of heavy shears, and tacks. Tack sizes

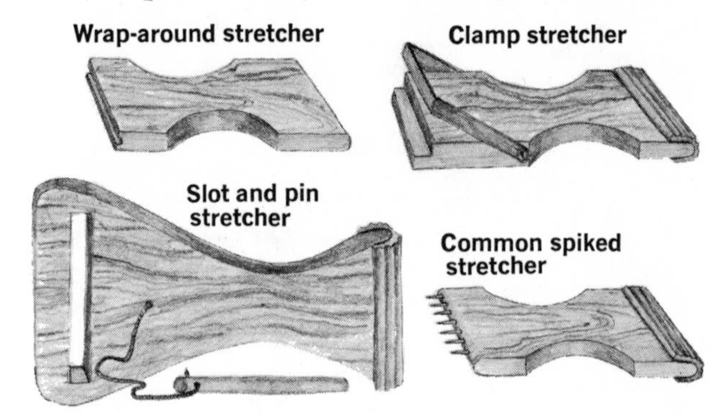

used for webbing seldom go below 8-ounce (#8) or above 16-ounce (#16). The most common size used is #12. Barbed webbing tacks most often are found in 12-ounce and 14-ounce sizes. They have, however, become increasingly difficult to find in many areas, so you may have to order them specially or make do with the next larger upholstery tack size.

To prevent confusion, front-to-back webbing and liner-to-rail webbing will be referred to as primary webbing; side-to-side webbing will be referred to as cross webbing.

Spacing, stretching, and tacking. It is always wise to mark off webbing strip locations (on the underside of the frame for a spring seat, or on top of the frame for a pad seat) with pencil or chalk. You can mark off a 4-foot stick with web spacing location (according to webbing width) so the frame can be marked with a minimum of fuss. Professional cabinetmakers long ago discovered that they make fewer mistakes in measurement if they use premarked gauge sticks rather than a yardstick.

Spacing between webs should be between ½ and 1 inch—¾ inch is a good standard to adopt. Never overlap parallel web edges—no usable strength is gained, and you get unsightly, lumpy tacking ends. Mark the front rail first, then mark locations directly opposite on the back rail, remembering that webbing should cross at right angles.

Do not cut webbing to length before tacking and stretching. To do so creates difficulties in stretching, since all stretchers—except the plier type—require excess webbing.

Fold over 1½ inches of the free webbing end and tack it to the frame ½ inch in from the outer edge with seven tacks in a staggered pattern to prevent splitting the wood. Guidelines drawn ½ inch from the outer edge of the frame are a great help. The ½-inch setback from the edge will prevent interference with cover applications. Occasionally you may have to use less than the ½-inch setback, but do so with some thought to preventing cover tacking problems.

To provide firm spring support, pull the webbing taut across the matching mark on the opposite rail. Place the cushioned end of the webbing stretcher against the outer side of the rail, at approximately a 30-degree angle to the free end of the stretcher (see photo). The exact method of gripping the webbing will depend on whether a spiked, slot-and-pin, or clamp stretcher is used.

With webbing gripped in the stretcher and held tight, hold the cushioned foot of the stretcher on the outer side of the rail with one hand and bear down on the gripping end with the heel of the other hand. In slow motion, you will feel the webbing tighten, then pop slightly as the stretcher reaches the horizontal position. Experiment a few times without final tacking to develop a feel for the angle at which you should start the stretcher to give you the firmest stretch without distorting the frame, popping the webbing tacks, tearing or breaking the webbing. You can test to see if desired firmness has been achieved by leaning on a webbing strip with the palm of your hand (much as you might lean heavily with one hand on a table top to reach something on the far side). The strip should give slightly but not enough to produce a noticeable bulge. You also can bounce the tack hammer head on the webbing to test for a drumhead sound and lively bounce.

Weak or faulty frames that distort when properly webbed must be reinforced by cross braces or rail thickening (see page 7).

With webbing properly stretched, drive four tacks

TACK WEBBING to front rail with seven tacks in staggered pattern. Folded end is ½ inch from rail edge.

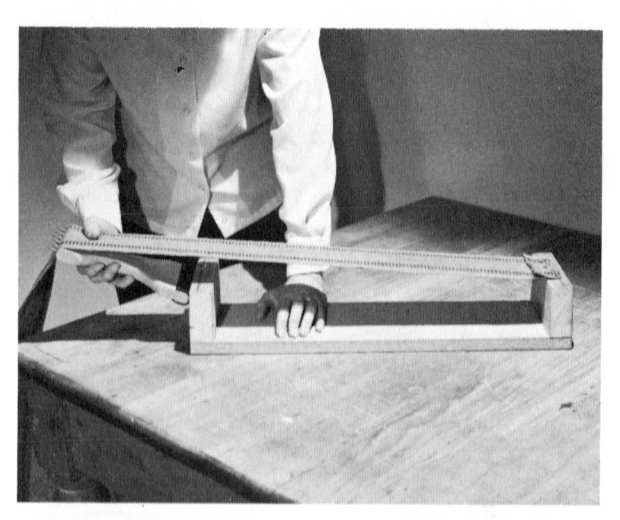

SPIKE STRETCHER through web at point that permits an angle of about 30 degrees between stretcher and rail.

PRESS DOWN on spiked end of stretcher until webbing tightens and snaps and the stretcher is horizontal.

spaced across the untacked end of the webbing and at least ½ inch from the outer rail edge. Release the stretcher, cut the webbing 1½ inches from the tack heads, fold the end over ½ inch from outer edge of rail, then tack it down with three tacks stagger-spaced between the original four.

Install all the primary (front-to-back) webbing in this fashion, then install the cross (side-to-side) webbing the same way. Interweave the cross and primary webbing for added support.

Slack webbing is occasionally used under padding for round or saddle-shaped seats, where the effect of sitting "into" rather than on a seat surface is desired. The webbing is tacked exactly as for taut seat webbing, except that webbing stretchers are not used and the webbing is allowed to fall in a natural curve to match the shape of the seat. Cross webbing is interwoven with the primary webbing and stitched to it to prevent side slipping and gaps.

Metal and wood webbing. Metal webbing is available in two basic forms: heavy preshaped steel wire or bar units with springs permanently attached (or corrugated to receive springs) and simple perforated steel strapping used largely to reinforce damaged or sagging jute webbing. Preformed steel wire or bar units are usually made to order for specific chair manufacturers in terms of size, gauge of wire, number of springs, and shape. If you are working on a piece with this type of webbing and it is in good shape or requires only local bar or wire straightening, you may either reuse it or remove and replace with jute webbing and coil springs.

WIRE WEBBING and spring unit was made to order for a manufacturer. Wire was used instead of twine.

Wooden webbing consists of individual hardwood or plywood slats running across the narrow dimension of the open frame, usually front to back, without the cross webbing commonly used with fabric webbing. It is generally used to reinforce bent spring bars. Occasionally metal strap cross webbing is also used to provide stress between the side rails equal to that exerted by the wood slats on the front and back rails. Plywood sheet webbing is best used under damaged jute webbing to produce a smoother surface.

Silencers are needed between metal webbing or wood and the bottom coils of springs. Jute webbing, several layers of folded burlap, or large balls of cotton stuffing are effective silencers. Without silencers, springs on wood will click or squeak.

Plywood sheet webbing is sometimes used to completely fill the frame opening and support coil spring, foam, or pad seats (same method used for reinforcing seat rails, see page 7). If coil springs are used, tack or staple the springs firmly to the wood and install silencers between the bottom coils.

Webbing backs and arms

Backs and arms designed for standard coil springs are webbed the same as seats except for two possible variations. Less expensive and lighter webbing (3-inch instead of 3½ or 4-inch) may be used, though it is wise to stay with heavy webbing on curved backs; and the webbing may be spread 2 to 4 inches apart as compared to the standard ¾-inch seat spacing.

Backs should be webbed with caution to determine the amount of stretcher pressure they will take. Some are relatively frail.

All back springs should fall on vertical webs. Where possible, install cross webbing so that it will fall under spring locations. For example, if nine equally-spaced springs are planned for a square back, there will be three vertical and three cross webs. Webbing must never cross divided back pull-through slats.

On flat backs and arms, interweave the primary and cross webs. On curved backs and arms, place the cross webs behind the primary webs. Vertical web spacing for curved backs will probably be considerably farther apart than for flat backs to allow clearance between the top coils of adjoining springs.

Backs that will have pad, foam, Marshall or inner-spring (see page 19) units should be webbed on the front side of the frame, since the frame depth is not needed to contain springs. If fairly wide web spacing is used, plan on stitching burlap over the web-

REPAIRING OR REPLACING FABRIC WEBBING

Sagging webbing may be the result of poor original stretching, loose or missing tacks, or damaged webbing. Rewebbing is so easy that except with relatively new webbing that was poorly stretched or one or two webs that have come loose, it is usually best to reweb the seat.

Special procedures must be followed for restretching and retacking webbing if it is cut too short for normal stretcher use. You can either add length by pinning an extra length of webbing to the short web and using a standard stretcher or use webbing pliers (also sold in art stores as canvas stretchers). Use a heavy, straight needle, regulator, upholsterer's pin, or nail to fasten webbing together. Where retacked webbing has come loose because tacks failed, metal strap webbing reinforcement may be advisable (see page 12).

Rewebbing through the underside of a seat involves a couple of preliminary steps. First remove the cambric bottom cover. Mark webbing location on rails, since new ones must be placed in exactly the same alignment. Remove web strips, one at a time, so you can see whether the tops of springs are still stitched to the burlap spring cover under the padding and tied to each other. If they have come loose, reposition the tops (usually you can see where by indentations in the burlap or by relative position and spacing to other springs), then stitch and tie to the burlap and to each other. If the cross ties between springs have broken and the spring is stiff enough to make reducing it to height difficult, hold it down with ties from its own top and bottom coils, then cross tie. The hold-down ties can be left in place.

Push the bottoms of the springs to one side so that the new webbing can be stretched without interference from spring pressure, then stretch and tack the new webbing in place. Relocate the spring bottoms on the new webbing, then stitch or use small hog rings to attach springs to webbing (see below).

bing to provide firmer support and an attachment base for the relatively denser packed Marshall units.

Attaching springs to webbing

Use a double pointed needle and stitching twine to stitch base coils of back and seat springs to webbing. The sketch below shows how to place the stitches. Start at a corner spring, tie the initial stitch, then proceed as shown, making four stitches per spring. Tie off the loose end of the twine. Position the springs so that the free or knotted side of the top coil is pointed to the center of the seat.

An alternate to stitching is using ½-inch hog rings to attach springs to webbing. Applied through the bottom of the webbing, they eliminate the possibility of cuts or scratches when dusting the finished piece.

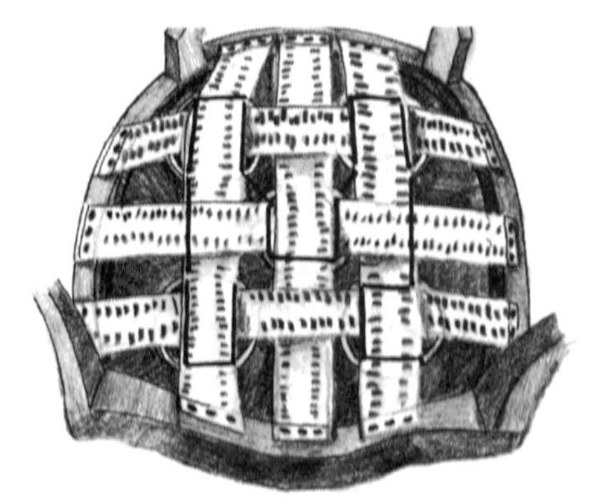

STITCH each coil spring to webbing at four points.

COIL COMPRESSION SPRINGS

Hardness of spring action is a function of the wire gauge, temper, and shape of the spring. The thicker the gauge of wire, the stiffer the spring. (Try to avoid using springs over #4 – they are too wobbly for most uses.)

Occasionally you will see three initials tacked to spring designations. "O.B.E." stands for "open both ends," K.O.E. for "knotted one end," and K.B.E. for "knotted both ends." Seat springs are normally O.B.E., back springs K.O.E., and cushion springs K.B.E. However, knotted springs–K.O.E. and K.B.E. –often are used in seats when available in desired height and hardness.

To test the spring action of used springs, stand them upright on a firm table top. Place the palm of your hand on the top coil of a spring and compress the spring with fast, continuous movements. If it compresses evenly with no side sway, it is still usable. Any spring that sways, folds in the middle, or otherwise deforms should be replaced. Very old springs once in a while have cracks which can break after retying and upholstering. Test them by grasping the top and bottom coils and twisting the ends back and forth through a half turn (180 degrees). Watch for

"RUN IN" a spring by forcing free end of top coil under next lower coil and working crossed point down the coils.

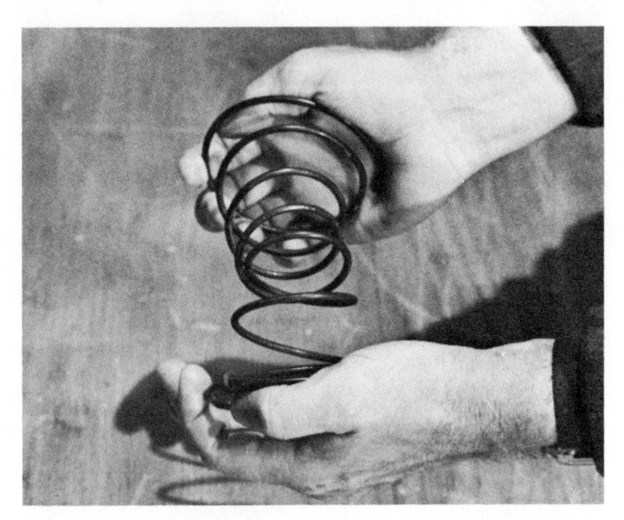

GRASP BOTH ENDS and use a rocking-twisting motion to work crossed point down, then back up the coils.

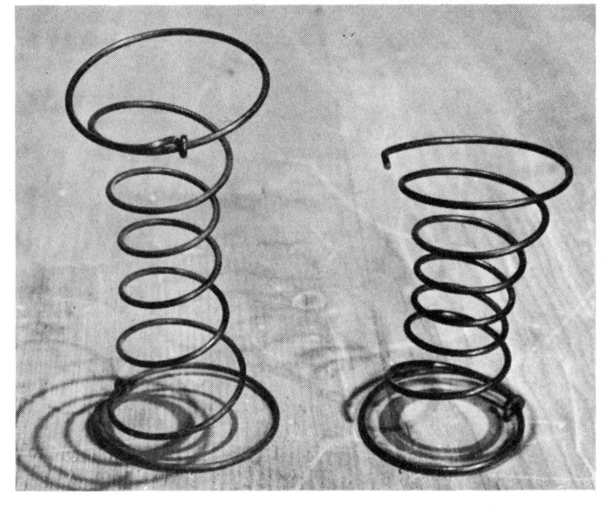

SHORTENED SPRING at right was identical to spring at left before it was run in. Note top is now unknotted.

cracks and deformation and listen for sharp cracking or crunching sounds. A cracked or brittle spring may break completely under this test.

If you can't find the exact size spring you want, there are three possible solutions. Use the next size taller and next grade softer and tie it down to the desired height (see opposite page); use the next size smaller and next grade harder and don't tie it down as tightly; or use the next larger size and next harder grade, then "run it in" before using.

"Running in" a spring is a handy way of shortening and softening it. Force end of top coil under the inside of the next lower coil, then manipulate the spring so the overlap point of the wires is "run-down" or "run-in" the whole length of the spring wire. Follow the steps in the pictures on this page. Note that if you run the wire one way, the contact point will run off the free end; the other direction runs it all the way down. If the spring is O.B.E. the process is simple; K.O.E. springs must be worked down from the unknotted end and back up; K.B.E. springs will require that the knot at one end be unwrapped or cut, then handled as K.O.E.

Tight-spring and spring-edge seats

Coil compression springs are tied in two basic configurations, for tight-spring and spring-edge seats. Springs for tight-spring seats are tied to produce either round or flat top surfaces and tied down tightly with spring twine to the frame edges. Spring-edge seats are flat and have heavy wire attached to the outer edge of the upper coils of the springs, which are more loosely tied to the frame edges.

Spring-edge seats are most often used to support loose spring or foam cushions. The springs that do not abut interfering members such as closed arms or backs are mounted as close as possible to the rail, and the top coil is moved forward to overlap the top of the rail. The rail should have folded burlap tacked to its inner surface if soft springs—with wide waists—are used. Otherwise squeaks can be caused by springs rubbing on the rail.

Tight-spring seats are most commonly found in occasional, side, pull-up, and less than fully upholstered chairs not having loose cushions. Because they are easier to construct than spring-edge seats, they are excellent first projects.

Springs for tight seats. When springs are being replaced, the original springs are often a good guide to gauge of wire, softness or hardness, and height of springs. If the old springs are obviously in bad condition or you are starting from scratch with a new frame, use the softest springs that will do the job and give the desired feel, appearance, and tautness or hardness. If the precise combination of softness and height is not available, use the next taller size and softer grade or the next shorter size and harder grade. Or use the next taller and harder spring and "run it in" as shown on the opposite page.

To determine tied height of springs, choose the desired height of the finished seat from the floor. Subtract 1 inch or more to allow for the specific padding thickness to be used, then subtract the distance from webbing to floor. The resulting figure is the tied height of the spring. For example, for an 18-inch-high seat with 1-inch-thick padding and webbing 12 inches from the floor, you would use a 5-inch spring for maximum resiliency or a 6 or 7-inch spring tied down to 5 inches for less resiliency.

Springs should not be tied down more than 2 inches below free-standing height. Resiliency resides primarily in the top 1 or 2 inches. Tying down any farther makes tying more difficult, produces harsh springing, and shortens the life of webbing, springs, tying twine, burlap, padding, and cover. Closed backs or arms dictate that seat springs be chosen so their tied height is the same as the distance from webbing to the pull-through liners or tacking strips on back and arms.

Open backs and arms require that seat springs be tied to at least the same height above the seat rail as the depth from the top of rail to the webbing, for example 3 inches above rail for a 3-inch rail, 4½ inches for a 4½-inch rail. Tying them closer to the rail would cause the springs to "bottom" against the tying twine and covering burlap when they are tacked to the rail tops, with resulting breakage and tearing. If short tying is absolutely necessary, tack the twine and covering burlap to the bottom of the rail or to a tacking strip glued in along the inner bottom lip of the rail.

Springs should not be tied higher than 1½ inches above the minimum height. Tying above this limit leads to problems in keeping the spring upright and usually leads to distortion under pressure. If for a specific effect (such as a stylized high-puff seat) it is absolutely necessary to tie above this maximum, consider double tying. Make the first ties to the center coils at the spring's narrow waist. Use the four-knot tie (see sketch), and slip-tack (see page 16) the twine to the *bottom* of the rail. Then tie top coils with either a four or eight-knot tie, adjust top of springs to height, and tack ends of twine to rail tops. Return to the midsection ties that were previously slip-tacked, pull twine taut—don't try to pull down the spring—and finish tacking.

Position springs in straight lines or rows. Out-of-line positioning results in zig-zag tying and wobbly-feeling seats. Place springs, if possible, at the webbing cross points so that the stitching or hog-ringing of the springs to the webbing also fastens the two webs together.

Space springs 2 inches from the inside of seat rails on exposed edges (edges without closed arms or back) and 1 inch from the inside of closed arm and back liners. They should be tied at least 1½ inches apart. However, for a given gauge and height, the farther apart the springs are spaced, the softer the seat will be. If more than 4 inches apart, the springs tend to distort under pressure.

Tying tight-spring seats. There are two basic patterns of tying springs for tight seats, but each pattern has both a name based on the number of *twines* crossing a given spring and a name based on the number of *knots* on the spring's circumference. The "two-way tie" and "four-way tie" refer to the very same tying methods as "four-way tie" and "eight-way tie." The illustrations below show that the two-way (twine) tie is identical to the four-way (knot) tie, and the four-way (twine) tie is identical to the eight-way (knot) tie. Further confusion is added by the descriptive terms "French," "diagonal," or "Union Jack" tie for the eight-knot tie and "English" for the four-knot tie.

Four-knot tie

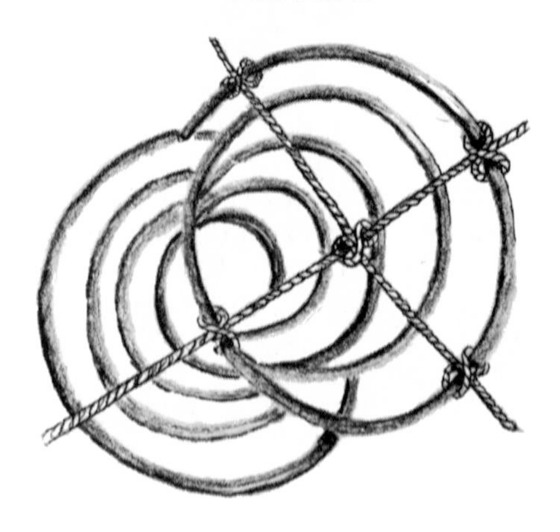

Eight-knot tie

If you use the words "twine" or "knot" in place of "way" you will be able to keep the confusion to a minimum when talking to furniture store or upholstery supply clerks. The terms four-knot and eight-knot ties will be used in this book.

A completed four-knot tie has four knots on the top coil of each spring. For each primary row of springs, a piece of twine is tacked to the chair rail to run across the top coil of each spring in the row to the opposite chair rail. The twine is tied in two places to each spring's top coil as it crosses the coil's circumference. Cross rows of twine are then tied to each spring top twice, and to the primary-row twine whenever two pieces of twine intersect.

The eight-knot tie starts the same as the four-knot tie but has additional pieces of twine running diagonally to the primary and cross rows so that two more pieces of twine—four more knots—cross over each spring. Knots are tied each place twine crosses twine as well as each place twine crosses a coil. The primary, cross, and diagonal ties form a pattern across each top coil similar to the cross pattern on the flag of Great Britain, giving this method the name "Union" or "Union Jack" tie.

The four-knot tie is the softer, more resilient method, and the eight-knot tie is stiffer and stronger. Round seats most often are tied with the four-knot tie.

Tight-spring seats are tied in either the "single-twine" or the "return" method. With single-twine tying, the springs nearest the seat rail are tied in the same way as the other springs (in the four-knot or eight-knot pattern) but the ends of the twine are then tacked to the rail. With return tying, the twine ends are returned from the rail to the outer spring to double-tie the rail-edge springs (see next page).

Precut the twine for single-twine tying in pieces as long as the distance between the chair rails to which the tie-down tacks will be attached. For return tying, cut the twine three times as long as the rail-to-rail distance. Cut as many lengths as there are primary rows and cross rows of springs, remembering that rail-to-rail distances for the cross ties may differ from those for the primary rows.

Tacking and knotting the twine. Twine can be fastened to the seat rail with either one or two tacks. Although some claim that single-tack tying is faster, many custom upholsterers and furniture restorers find the twin-tack system simple, little if any slower, and far more reliable. Tack the twine for the center row of springs first, working from back to front rail.

The single-tack method consists of slip-tacking (driving a tack only partway into the rail) a single tack, looping an overhand knot (first half of a granny or square knot) over the tack, tightening the knot, then driving the tack in to anchor the knot.

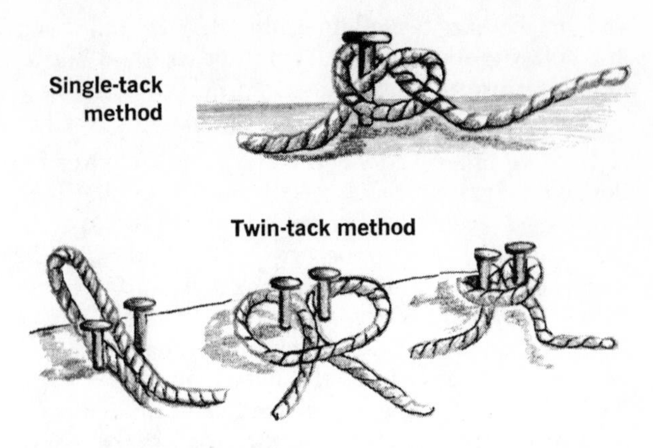

Single-tack method

Twin-tack method

The twin-tack method is to slip-tack a pair of tacks so that they stand with heads barely a single twine's width apart. Loop the twine and pass the loop between tacks, flip the loop over and around the two tack heads, draw the twine tight, and drive the tacks in to lock the twine (see sketch above).

Many upholsterers and most beginners find it easiest to use single turns or loops to tie the twine to a spring. This lets you work the coil forward or back along the tightened and tacked-down twine to

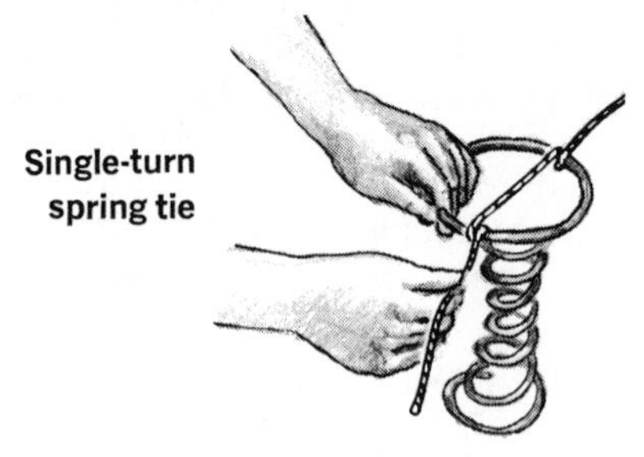

Single-turn spring tie

ensure upright spring placement. The disadvantages of this system are that slippage can occur in use and a break anywhere on a twine will allow all the half hitches to work loose and the springs to shift.

Spring or clove hitch knots provide a much more permanent tie, since they do not loosen in chain reaction if the twine breaks. Tie a knot at each point the twine crosses a spring coil and other twine.

Spring or clove hitch tie

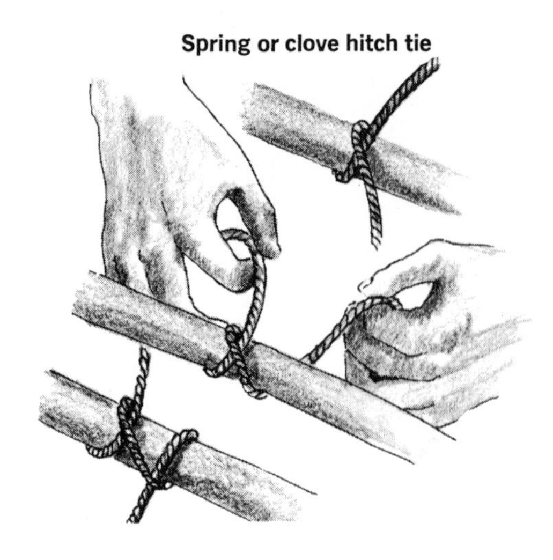

When you end a tie twine at a coil an additional half hitch or two makes the loose end more secure. An added insurance is to use a drop or two of white glue on the last half of the final tying-off clove hitch.

There is one problem for the beginner in using the all clove or spring-hitch system. It is practically impossible to adjust the position of the springs along the twine once it is taut. However, with a little practice you can start with twine tacked to the rear rail and locate and tie each knot correctly before tying the next one. An alternate method that works well for some is to start at the center spring in the row and then work toward both ends of the row. Tie the knots so that each spring's top coils are spaced exactly over its bottom coil or very slightly off-center toward the center of the seat to allow for possible stretching during the process of pulling the springs down to height and tie-tacking. When the coils are tied, pull down to the right height and tack twine ends to rail. Repeat the process for all rows parallel to the center row. Start the cross ties on the center row at right angles to the primary rows, being sure to tie knots where twine crosses twine as well as coils. Watch that tied primary rows are not pulled out of line when cross ties are pulled taut. Be certain that the cross ties are not pulled down so tight that the tautness of any of the primary ties is decreased.

Return tying for tight-spring seats. When return tying is used for round seats, the outermost edge of the top coil of each spring is left knot-free and the twine is knotted to the next lower coil. The springs are then pulled down to height, and the twine is looped and locked around the tacks. The free end is returned to the spring, knotted around the free edge of the upper coil, then tied off next to the first knot previously made on the inner edge of the top coil.

Return tie for spring-edge seat

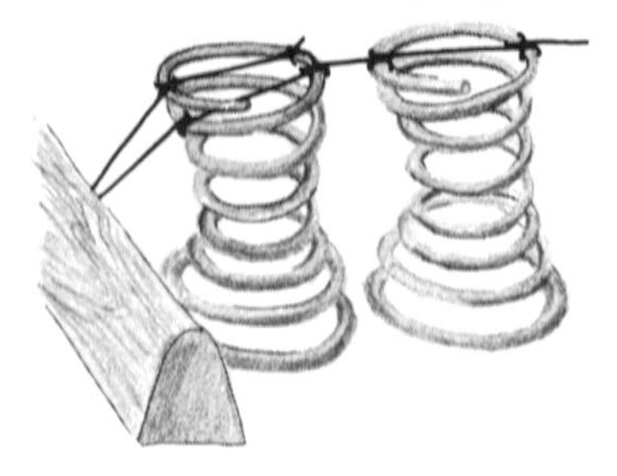

Many workers continue the twine to the near side of the top coil on the adjoining spring. A half hitch can be added on the other side of the original knot as anti-slip insurance. Varying the length of the return tie between tacks and free edge of the top coil allows you to vary the seat shape considerably. The double tie on each outer spring lessens the likelihood of twine breakage between spring and rail.

For flat seats tied by the return twine method, the basic tie may drop as low as the second coil from

ROUND SEAT model shows non-return (single-twine) tying. Felted cotton balls have been used as silencers.

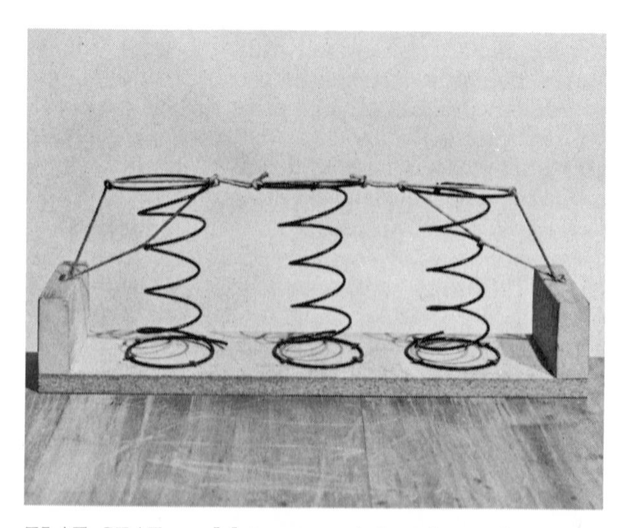

FLAT SEAT model is return-tied; only single turn is used on lower coil. Springs are tacked to wood base.

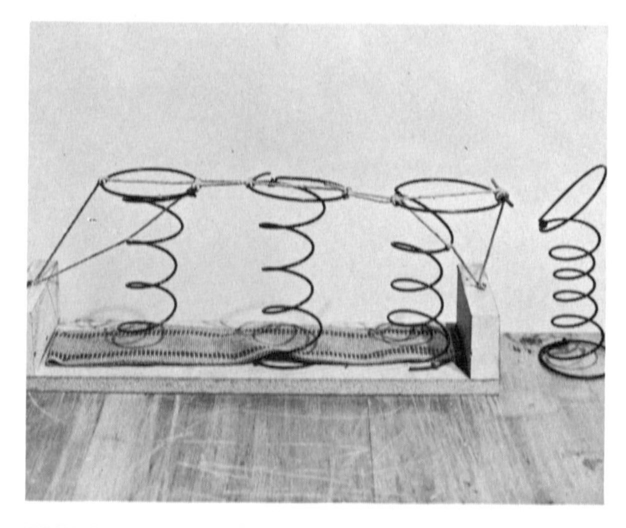

SPRING-EDGE model shows edge wire, webbing used as spring silencer. Tilt-topped spring sample is at right.

the top on the outer springs. The return twine is knotted on the free coil edge to hold it perfectly in line with its inner edge, producing a flat surface.

Tying spring-edge seats. Spring-edge seats are tied the same as flat seats except that the springs along the rail edge are placed as close to the rail as possible and the top coils are enlarged and bent forward and up so the outer edge of the top coil will be in line with the outer face of seat rail when the coil is held flat by the return twine. The rail-edge springs should be shaped before being stitched to the webbing.

To enlarge the top coil of a spring that already has the top end of the coil knotted or wrapped around the second coil, loosen the knot with pliers or tube-type wire bender and slide it farther down the coil. The top coil will become enlarged and tend to jut out on the side opposite the wire knot or wrapping. Grasp the jutting edge and bend it upward until it stands by itself at a 45-degree angle. Fasten the spring to the webbing with stitching or hog rings with the bent-up spring coil over the seat rail. Return-tie the spring so that the enlarged and bent-up top coil is flat and the outer edge is in vertical alignment with the outer surface of the seat rail.

If the spring's top coil is not self-knotted, use a wire bender to loop or wrap the end around the second coil. Then enlarge and bend up the top coil as for the self-knotted spring.

Before tying the spring to the rail, take a 9-gauge wire and duplicate the shape of the open seat rail. Before installing this wire, work it free of twists so that it will lie flat. Bend the free ends down to prevent damage to the seat cover.

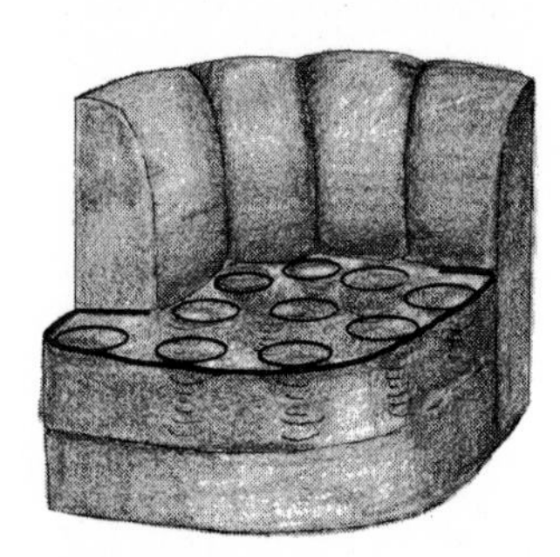

Half T-cushion platform seat

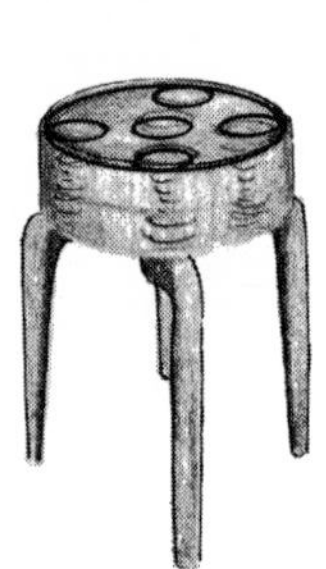

Round stool seat

Open-arm chair

This edge wire can be bent by sliding a pair of 10-inch lengths of ⅛-inch galvanized (¼-inch inside diameter) steel pipe over the wire and using them as levers to bend the wire. To form shallow or large-radius curves, place the wire on a block of hardwood and strike it sharply with a hammer. Each strike will produce a small increase in the bend. An increased number of hammer strikes over a short length will produce greater bending.

If the design of the piece requires that the ends of the edge wire are to be attached to the frame, do so before attaching it to coil springs. Use one of the clips, shown on page 20, or fold a piece of webbing around the wire and tack the ends to the frame with three nails. Then fasten the edge wire to springs with spring clips or stitching twine. There are special pliers that enable you to fasten the clips in one motion, but each tab can be successfully closed using standard pliers. The sketch below shows how to use stitching to lash twine edge wire to springs. Springs that touch the edge wire when properly positioned must be lashed at all points of contact. For instance, an edge wire on a T-cushion

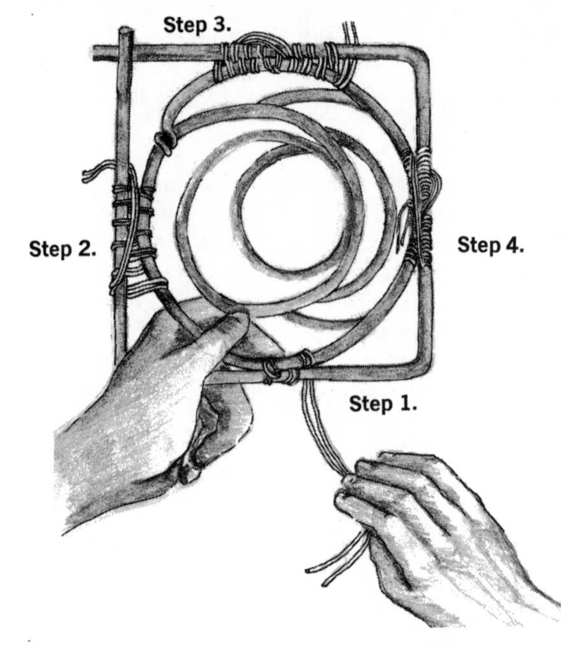

support could require lashing at three distinct points for a single spring. Be certain when lashing springs to the edge wire that they are in line with the springs they will be tied to in the primary and cross rows, so that tying will not distort the springs. Diagonal ties need not be return tied.

Tying coil spring backs

Back springs on most frames, whether round, flat, or spring-edged, are tied almost exactly as seats are. Softer, lighter-gauge springs are used, with both ends knotted (K.B.E.), and placed with 2 to 4 inches between each spring. Softer tying twine is also used. Only four-knot tying is used, and intermediate or filler ties often are knotted from twine to twine between springs to provide a finer-meshed supporting network for the stuffing. On spring-edge backs the filler ties may be tied off at the edge wire or continue to the rail.

Marshall or pocketed innerspring cushion units are occasionally used for backs.

Round or curved contoured chair backs are sprung over vertical webbing only. Stitch coil springs to webs in vertical rows with 2 to 3-inch vertical spacing between springs and 2 to 3-inch horizontal spacing between the top coils of adjacent springs. Tie the springs to the correct height in vertical rows only—horizontal ties would interfere with shaping.

Parallel ties for springs of barrel back chair

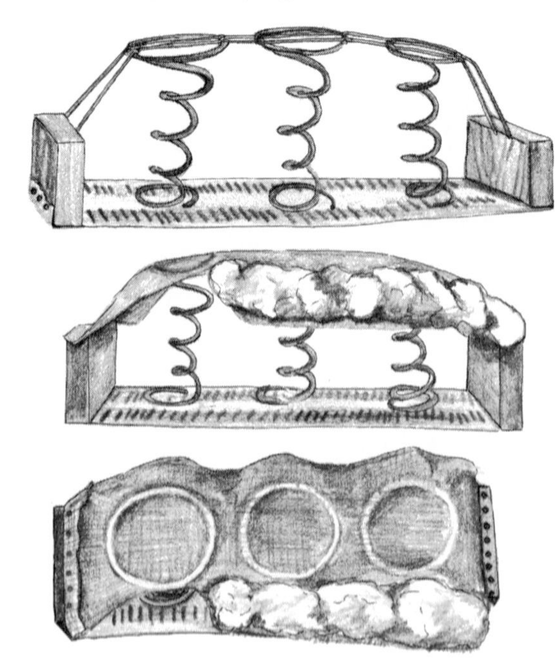

For greater stability some upholsterers use two parallel ties run slightly each side of center on the coils, and the coil-to-rail ties are spread slightly apart for tacking.

Though a single length of burlap could be tucked and tacked over and between the springs, use separate strips for each row of springs until you gain some experience. Cut burlap strips long enough to cover a specific vertical row of springs, with enough extra length to reach top rail and liner and extra width to permit tacking to the top rail and the liner midway between the adjoining spring rows.

Draw the burlap taut over the springs and tack the burlap's vertical centerline to the top rail and liner on the centerline of the spring row. Draw the burlap down between spring rows, stretch tautly, and tack to the center point between rows on top rail and liner. Repeat on each side and for each row.

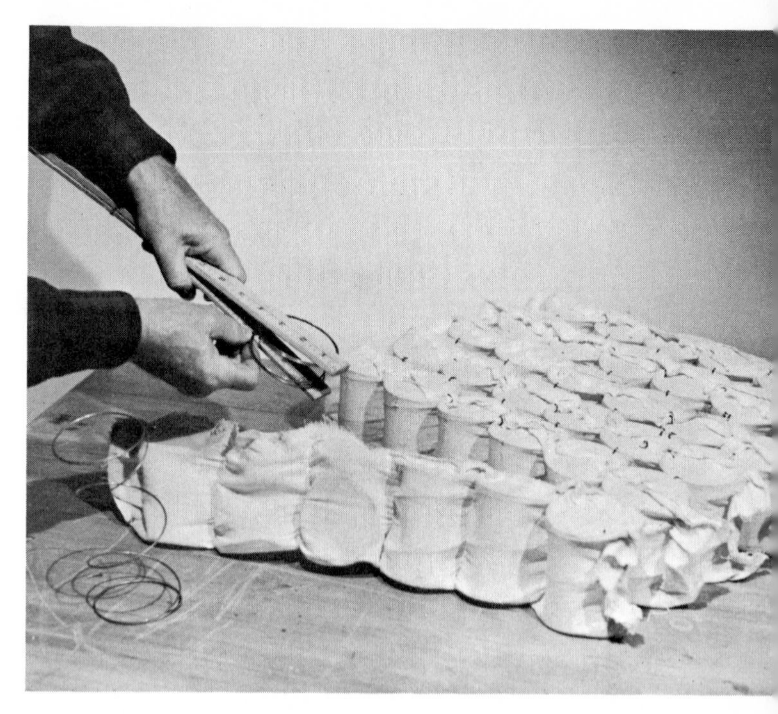

COMPRESS SPRINGS between wooden strips and fit sideways into Marshall unit. Sew pockets, turn springs.

Draw edges of burlap taut over top rail and liner, then tack. Stitch together the edges of burlap between the spring rows to keep stuffing materials out of spring and webbing space. Stitch the burlap to the top coils of the springs, using three stitches per coil (see page 23). Cut off any excess burlap at top and bottom rails.

Pocket or Marshall springs

Pocket or Marshall springs are small coil-type cushion springs that are individually enclosed in muslin or burlap pockets which are in turn edge-stitched together in groups or sets for use in mattresses, pillows, and some chair backs. These units may be purchased ready-made in a wide variety of shapes, according to the number and placement of pockets and strips. The springs themselves are generally 3 inches in diameter and vary from 3½ inches high for innerspring cushions to 6 inches for chair backs.

When repairs are necessary and the springs themselves are in good shape, you can simply make new pockets. If standard 3-inch-diameter and 3½-inch-high springs are used, cut 15-inch-wide strips of muslin or burlap. Fold the strip double to make a 7½-inch-wide strip. Sew one 7½-inch end closed and run seams parallel to this stitching at 9¾-inch intervals to form pockets. Since springs vary, it is wise to insert a spring in the first pocket to check for fit before sewing the rest of the seams. The pocket should be tight enough to prevent the spring from turning over, but not tight enough to restrict free spring compression.

Insert springs into the pockets, and sew the length closed. Sewing this seam will be easier if you compress the springs and insert them into the pockets sideways, then manipulate them into final position after you have sewn the edge closed.

The pocket strips can then be folded and assembled into almost any shape. Stitch the top and bottom coils of adjoining springs together with a curved needle and stitching twine, using the lock stitch shown on page 23. Tie off twine ends securely. An alternate to stitching is to use ½-inch hog rings or clinch staples at each spring-to-spring junction.

LOW PROFILE SPRINGS

Sagless or zig-zag wire springs are the most common low profile springs used in furniture. In spite of their sinuous shape, they depend on compression for the spring effect.

Sagless wire springs can be purchased in precut lengths with ends bent to fit retaining clips. Bulk rolls more than 100 feet long are available and can be cut to the desired length with bolt cutters, a triangular file, or a fine-toothed hacksaw. Ends can be bent by using a wire-bending jig or by gripping the wire in a vise and striking it with a hammer. Spring ends should be cut so that each end points to the same side of the spring to provide facing loops for cross connecting with small coil springs or wire clips.

Clips and hinge links for zig-zag spring construction

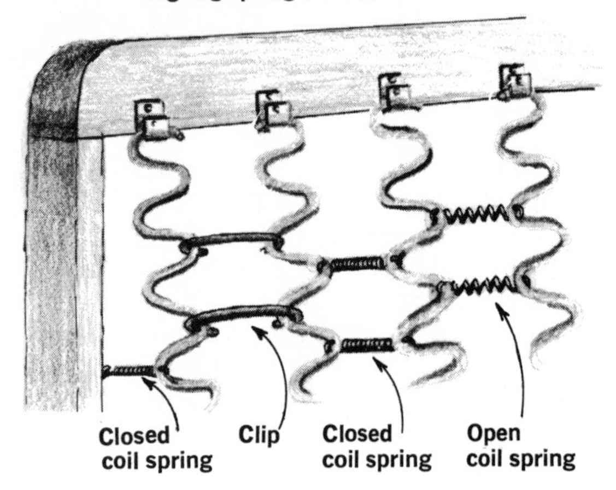

The spring strips are arched between front and back seat rails or back rail and liner with bent ends alternating right and left and attached to the frame. The illustration that follows shows hinge links and clips for various shapes and uses. Occasionally frames will have to be reinforced to take the strong front-to-back-rail and top-rail-to-liner pull of these springs (see page 7).

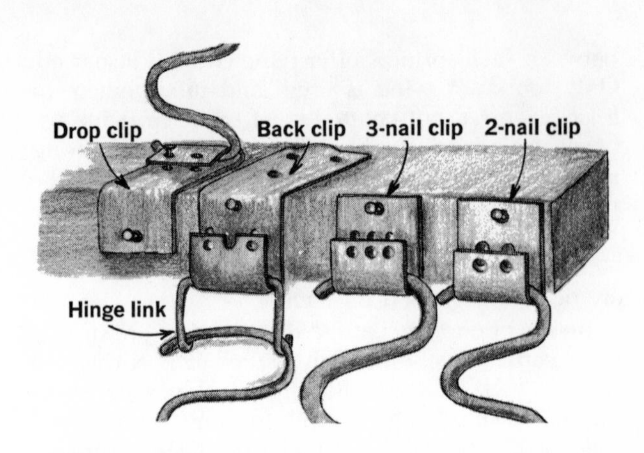

Small close-wound helical (coil) springs are used to tie the two outer zig-zag springs to the side rails of the frame and between spring strips to provide unified spring action and support for stuffing. Small open-wound helical springs are used to tie together the zig-zag strips in backs and provide stuffing support. For both seat and back use helical springs 2 inches shorter than the center-to-center distance between the spring clips. Use a 2-inch helical for 4-inch spacing and a 4-inch helical for 6½-inch spacing (ignore fractions).

Spacing and shaping of zig-zag springs can be confusing for the beginner. To measure the length of zig-zag springs, always work on a solid surface. Hold the free end of the wire beside or on one end of a tape or yardstick, then force the roll of spring wire open until the spring lies flat on the surface. (Wrapping a tape measure around rolled-up wire to measure it can give misleading results.) If the desired length falls so that the cut end of the spring would point opposite to the starting end, make the cut at the next longer bend (not the next shorter bend). Repeat for all springs of the same length.

Seat spring spacing should be 4 to 5 inches between spring centerlines. Spacing between outer springs and arm posts or end rails may vary between 1½ and 3 inches.

Maximum resiliency is obtained with convex spring arc heights of 2 inches to 2¼ inches, though arc heights as low as 1¼ inches are common where an extremely low profile and a fairly stiff seat are desired. A good standard to work by is the "normal" arc which varies between 1½ and 2 inches when the spring length (measured flat) is exactly the same as the inside dimension between front and back rail. The shorter the front-to-back dimension, the nearer the arc is to 1½ inches; the longer the dimension, the nearer the arc approaches 2 inches. For example, if an 11-inch spring is used for an 11-inch front-to-back seat dimension, the arc is close to 1½ inches; if a 24-inch spring is used in a 24-inch seat, the arc is closer to 2 inches.

If you are repairing a piece and an extra ¼-inch arc height would help, or if extra resiliency is desired, hinge links can be used. Links are used at the rear spring clips. By adding length to the spring they add ¼ inch arc height. If extra resiliency without increased arc height is the aim, use hinge links but reduce the length of the spring by approximately 1 inch.

If you need a specific spring arc height required for design effect, make a pattern from a strip of stiff cardboard – tacking strips are ideal. With spring clips in place, slip-tack the cardboard strip alongside the rear clip, slip a nail through the clip's loop so that it passes over the cardboard strip, and mark the cardboard at this point. Then pass the cardboard strip under a nail inserted through the loop of the front clip. Manipulate the strip until the desired arc height is obtained, and mark the strip at the point it reaches the front clip's loop. Then use the cardboard as a yardstick for spring measurement.

You also can use a length of spring to determine the desired length. Clip one end to the back rail, bring the other end to the front rail clip, adjust for arc height, and mark the spring for cutting.

STRAP AND COIL SPRINGS used as loose cushion seat support are attached to frame with heavy screw eyes.

Clip installation

Clip positioning for low-profile springs in seats with front and rear rails of equal length is determined by the normal 4 to 5-inch spacing between spring centerlines of adjoining rows. However, when the seat has one spring-bearing rail shorter than the other, clip spacing on the shorter rail will have to be reduced to permit springs to be attached without touching each other. Where possible make spacing adjustments between clips for the outer rows of springs, leaving as many of the clips as possible for the center rows normally spaced. If one rail's length

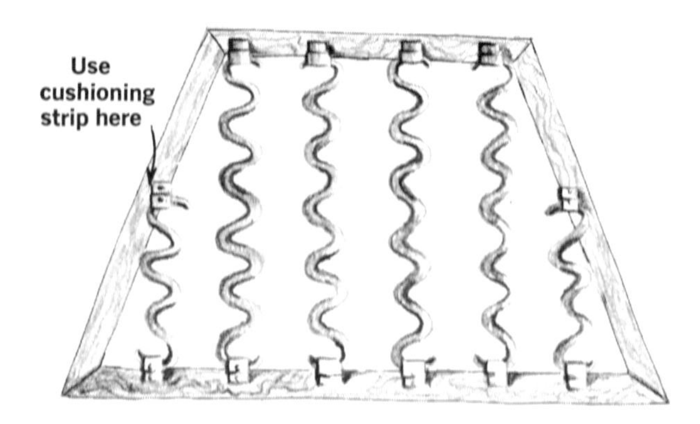

is severely limited, it may be necessary to bring the springs to the tapering side rails to keep them from touching. In this case, consider using rubber, burlap, or webbing cushioning strips between springs and rail overlaps to prevent contact noises.

Mount clips as shown in the drawings on the opposite page. The looped ends of spring clips are allowed to hang ⅛ inch over the inside frame edge to provide freedom of movement for the springs. The right angled clips can be used to drop the spring hinge points over the frame edge.

Hold the clip in place with a single nail, insert spring or hinge link, then drive in remaining nails. Where a single nail passes through two holes, the bottom hole is larger. The larger hole permits you to angle the nail toward the center of the rail without distorting the clip. Use ¾ to 1-inch barbed, cement-coated, ridged, or screw-type nails with heavy heads for nailing spring clips. Ordinary household nails and tacks simply don't hold up well under pressure.

Strap and coil tension springs

The springs so often used in fold-out beds are probably the most common version of strap and coil tension springs. They are simply straps of sheet metal, wire, wire or grommet-edged canvas or burlap, or even rope, made several inches shorter than the frame opening (running length and width) and attached at each end to the frame by close-wound coil springs which are just tight enough to hold the strips flat but without any noticeable opening between the spring coils.

Where a wire or grommet-edged cloth platform is used, springs may be attached on all four sides or on only three, with one edge tacked to the front rail. Always use a protective cover over coil extension springs or they will bite into top cushions and rapidly cause wear.

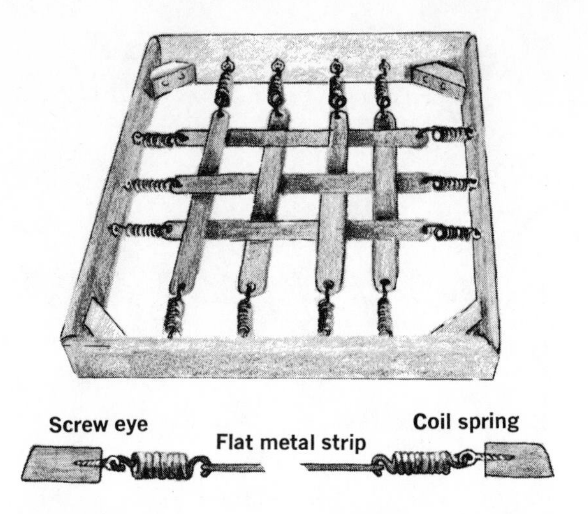

INTERWEAVE steel strap springs to make platform.

The coil springs for strap-spring units may be attached to the frame with the same kind of clips used for zig-zag springs, with screw eyes set into the inner edges of the frame, with metal plates, or with retaining pins and slots routed into the rails.

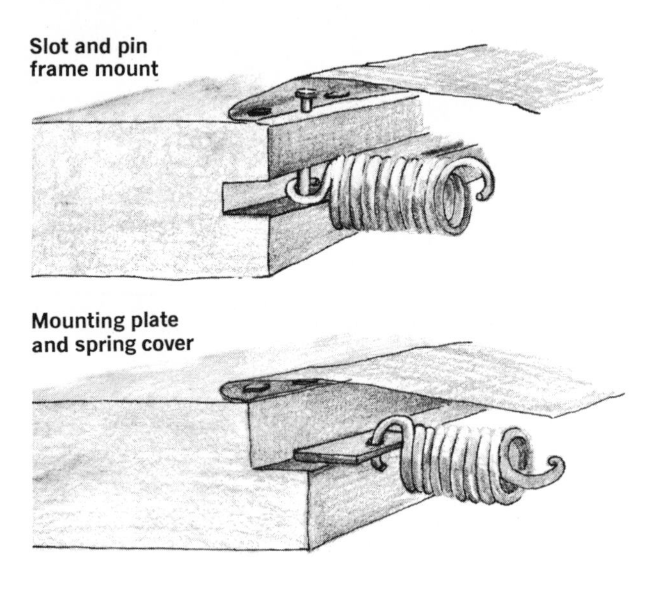

Rubber strap or web springs

The reinforced rubber webbing so often found under the seat cushions of Scandinavian imports has more than enough resiliency to provide excellent springing. This material is available in either precut lengths with clips attached or in bulk rolls for either tacking or using with clips. Cut slots into the frame to fit the specific clips used.

Installing rubber web springs with tacks requires the use of webbing pliers or other webbing stretcher. Stretching techniques are similar to those for jute

RUBBER WEBBING has mounting clips that fit slots in seat rails. Ends could be tacked like jute webbing.

webbing installation (see page 11), except that you will have a highly resilient material to stretch.

Clip installation requires that the combined length of the cut rubber web and the two end clips be shorter than the distance between the attaching slots in the frame. Exactly how much shorter it must be depends on the width, thickness, and stretch of the specific brand of rubber web used. When installed, the webbing should bear seated weight with a maximum of 1-inch depression.

Cable springs

The continuous-loop, rubbery, ropelike springs that have become increasingly popular for use in the seats of Scandinavian designs were at one time simply sophisticated rubber bands, but now they are thin coil extension springs of wire with rubber or plastic covers. The ends are joined with special connectors which screw into the open coil ends. Furniture stores are beginning to carry replacement parts for their own stock, but these springs are still fairly hard to obtain.

In homemade furniture the most common problem with cable springs is making the curved retainer grooves in the frame. Using a router is the easiest way to make them. If you do not have access to a router, use a hand coping saw or electric saber, band, or jig saw to make the retainer grooves. Cut out enough scalloped strips and scallop cutouts to glue to the top of the front and back seat rails and a pair of plain strips of equal height for the side rails. Glue them down and loop the springs over the scallop cutouts.

SPRING COVERS

A fabric cover is needed over all springs to keep stuffing materials out of the spring spaces. Use heavy burlap and cover all springs where padding is to be used.

Determine burlap size by measuring over the tied springs to the outer edges of the tacking surface of the rails and liners. Add 2 generous inches at each edge where edge rolls are not required. For each edge requiring a handmade edge roll, allow extra burlap (see discussion on pages 25 and 26).

Draw the burlap tightly over the springs and slip-tack it at the centers of front, back, and sides. Pull the burlap smoothly to back post, arm stump, or other interfering members, then mark, cut, and fold it to fit. Slip-tack it tautly in place. Stitch the burlap to the top coils of springs with stitching twine and 2 or 3-inch curved needle, using the three-stitch pattern and lock stitch.

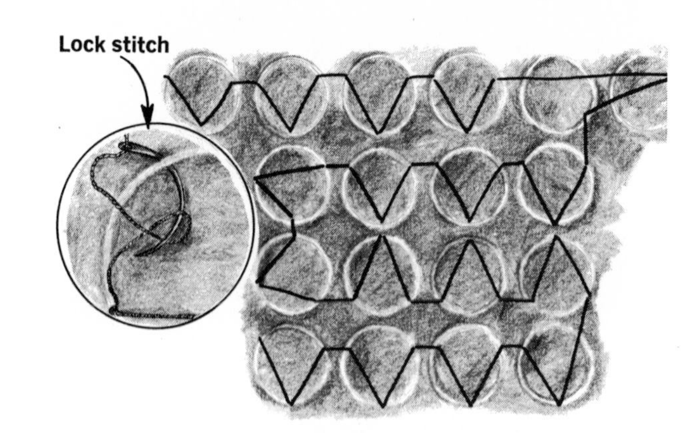

Remove the slip tacks, holding the burlap in place. Retack the burlap 1½ inches apart, leaving a little slack so that the tying twine takes all the strain of the springs and the burlap merely keeps the stuffing materials out.

TACKING TOOLS AND METHODS

A tack hammer will be your most frequently used upholstery tool, so it is important to choose one carefully. The tack hammer is used to smooth fabric and shape stuffing as well as to drive tacks. It has a magnetic face for picking up tacks; a hammer with an unslotted magnetic face is easiest to keep clean and free of stray metal chips or tacks which could damage covers when the hammer head is used to smooth fabric. A good hammer feels well balanced and turns easily in your hand.

Practice tacking on a scrap piece of wood (preferably medium-hard hardwood such as alder, ash, birch, gum, poplar, or soft maple) on which you have penciled one curved line and one straight line. Pick up single tacks with the magnetic hammer face and use the non-magnetic face to drive them ½ inch apart along the lines. Use a variety of tack sizes.

Tacks should be spaced just far enough apart to hold fabric securely and smoothly—½ to 1½ inches, depending on the stiffness and weight of the fabric. Thin silks tacked to a curved exposed wood edge often require tacks every ½ inch, or even closer, to produce a smooth, strong edge. Thick leather or plastic covers usually require tacks only every 1½ inches along straight, hidden edges.

Slip tacks are often used in upholstery. These are tacks driven only half or two-thirds their length into the wood frame for temporary tacking. They can be removed easily by using ripping tools (wood chisels with offset handles) or by striking them sideways with the tack hammer.

Tacked seams and welt can be strengthened with tacking strips, ⅜ to ½-inch-wide strips of cardboard placed over seam allowances. Tack through strip and fabric; tacks are seldom required closer than every 1 inch. Tacking strips are used in blind tacking to produce invisibly tacked edges (see sketch).

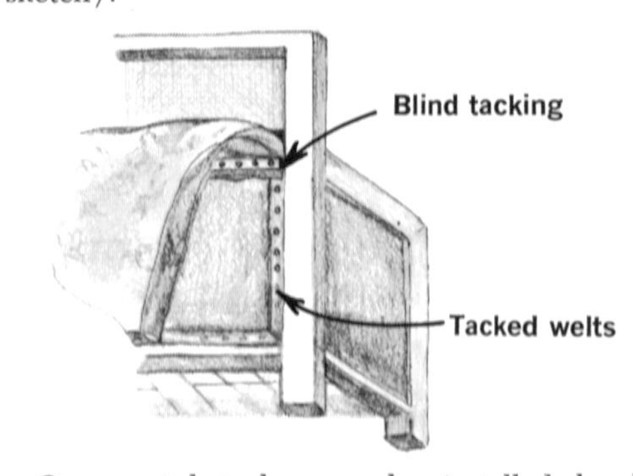

Ornamental tacks may be installed head-to-head, or you can space them apart. Accurate spacing can be achieved by using a marked strip of cardboard under the heads, between the tacks, and slip-tacking (see sketch on page 16). Drive the tacks in when all have been located correctly.

Edge Softening and Shaping

Upholstered furniture would be extremely angular and uncomfortable and would need frequent padding and cover repair if it were not for the use of edge rolls and spring-edge rolls. These rolls provide a softer edge for padding, covers, and people to bear against, and they help contain stuffing materials. They also provide a firm extension for raising supporting rails to spring height. Spring-edge rolls are used on springs, and edge rolls are used on all frame members and webbed platforms.

Use commercial edging for your first project or until you are familiar with the techniques used in making your own. When the correct commercial size is available you can usually save both time and money by using it. If the size is unavailable, make your own by following the methods detailed in the following discussion.

The roll size required depends on the depth of padding to be used. The ¼ and ⅜-inch rolls are used with the thin padding of severely-firm modern pieces or any of the very thin paddings used for appearance only. Padded arm tops, backs, and seats often use ½ and ¾-inch rolls. Thicker backs and seats make use of 1 and 1½-inch ready-made rolls. Rolls larger than 1½-inch in diameter, such as those used as rail extensions, have to be handmade and stitched to shape.

Rubberized hair is sometimes used as a combined padding and edge softener for boxy edge shapes.

COMMERCIAL EDGE ROLLS

Ready-made edge rolls are available in sizes from ¼ to 1½ inches, though they are often hard to find locally in sizes other than ½, ¾, and 1 inch except on special order. They are usually made of burlap or felt over rolled burlap, paper, rope, cotton, or other fibers. You can purchase them by the foot or in coils. Avoid the softer edge rolls—they tend to pack down and lose shape. Firmer rolls wear better.

Choose the roll size to match the thickness of the padding on the primary (more important) surface next to the edge to be softened. The abutting secondary surface will usually have thinner padding, or none at all. The attaching lip and the greater part of the roll rest on the primary surface with a small overhang over the secondary face. Where both adjoining surfaces require equal padding thickness, make a ¼-inch chamfer (bevel) on the frame edge, use the next larger roll, and tack it with the roll centered on the chamfer.

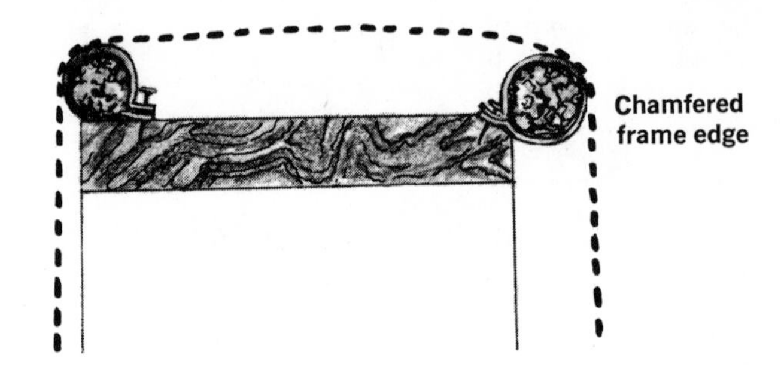

Tack (see above) or back-stitch ready-made rolls to the primary surface so close to the roll, through the lip, that the tacks or stitches actually catch some of the shaping fiber. Tacking farther out on the lip creates a wobbly, useless edge roll which will pull back from the edge. Spring-edge rolls should have extra retaining stitches going through the back half of the roll down to the edge wire and around the wire.

When tacking a ready-made roll, shape a recess at the tacking point by giving a couple of sharp tack-hammer raps exactly where you intend to tack. Drive the tacks at a slight angle into the roll. Use tacking strips—½-inch-wide stiff cardboard strips—to reinforce loosely stitched rolls; tacks spaced 1½ inches apart are adequate. Without tacking strips, space tacks at 1-inch intervals or closer.

Curved edges may require some mitering or pleating of the roll lip. Right-angle corners will require either mitering, with cuts made into the roll itself as well as the lip, or butt joints. Some people feel that

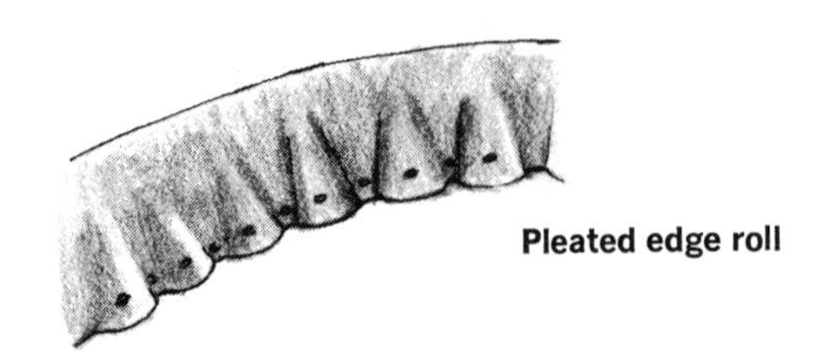

Pleated edge roll

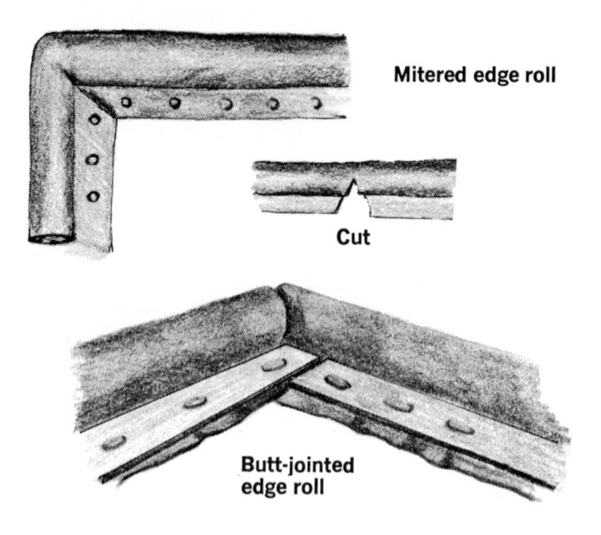

butt-joined corners tack down more firmly than mitered corners on ready-made rolls.

Regular tacking strips can be used almost up to the edge-roll corners. Shape corner strips by hand from upholsterer's chipboard to fit the corners.

PREBUILT EDGE ROLLS shown are, from left, paper-stuffed (spring-edge roll), fiber-stuffed, rolled burlap.

HANDMADE EDGE ROLLS

Edge rolls can be formed by hand anywhere burlap can be stitched or tacked. Cut and stitch or tack the burlap parallel to the threads so that raveling is minimized and the lengthwise threads can be used as a guide for shaping and sizing. When you stuff the roll, remove any oversize pieces of filling or any foreign particles which could deform the final shape.

Small edge rolls

Edge rolls 1½ inches or less in diameter are usually made with essentially round cross-section shapes. Cut strips of burlap four times as wide as the desired roll diameter. The strips may simply be extensions of burlap used to cover webbing or springs.

Tack the burlap so its lengthwise threads are parallel to the frame edge. Since butt-joining at corners is difficult when loose fiber fillings are used, either place strips so that they round corners or provide adequate overlap of adjoining strips. Overlap adjoining strips on straight edges at least 1½ inches, somewhat more on curves.

To round corners with continuous strips, grasp the free edge of the strip in line with a 45° diagonal at the corner, hold it stretched out level with the tacking surface, then form a pleat at the corner for continued tacking around the corner. (Without a pleat, tacking would necessitate severe flattening of the roll.) Use #4 or #6 tacks and tacking strips to tack the first edge. Use #6 or #8 tacks to close the roll and catch some of the fiber filling to minimize fiber shifting.

Fillers for hard rolls can be tightly rolled or twisted kraft or crepe paper, smooth-surfaced rope, or tow. For medium-hard or soft rolls, they can be rolled stitched burlap or canvas, soft smooth rope, moss, or hair. Medium-hard to hard rolls generally are more durable than soft ones and provide better support for covers.

Rolled fabric or paper and rope or string are virtually self-forming, and the burlap strip is merely used as a tacking case (see above). Loose fiber roll filling such as tow, moss, or hair requires more manipulation. After tacking the burlap to the frame edge, place a row of fiber over the tacks and experimentally roll the burlap up and over the filling to determine how much fiber is needed for the desired size and firmness.

Start at the center of each edge and work toward each corner, placing the necessary amount of filling on the burlap strip. Draw burlap tightly over filling and shape into an even round roll, driving tacks into the free edge so that the tacks pierce some of the lower portion of filling. The tacks should be next to or between the initial tacks.

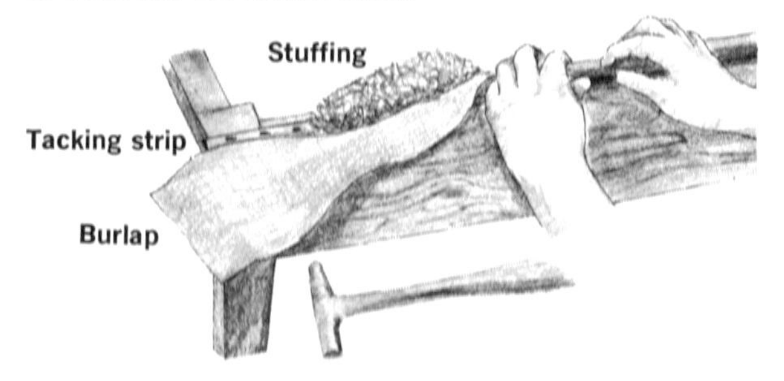

STITCH CORNERS closed; otherwise they will soon lose their shape, and loose stuffing may leak out.

Remember to use lengthwise threads in the burlap as a guide when forming rolls. If the original edge was tacked along a thread guide line, a roll of uniform size will be formed if you finish-tack along a parallel thread. If a tapered roll is desired, use the parallel thread as a taper guide.

After forming the rolls between corners, fill the rolls at the corners, keeping the same shape, size, and overhang as elsewhere. Then fold under the excess material, pleat, and tack in place. A shaped corner tacking strip is handy here. Use a small curved needle and stitching twine to close the pleat.

Use a stuffing regulator, ice pick, or heavy needle to work out minor lumps and hollows under the burlap. Tack open ends of roll to any abutting frame member, such as arm stumps and back posts, to keep filling from coming out through open ends.

Large edge rolls

Stitched edge rolls for platform, tight-spring, and spring-edge use are virtually identical. The differences are mainly in the supporting surface—horizontal for platform and spring-edge, semi-vertical for tight-spring edges.

Any edge roll over 1½ inches high should be made so that its cross section is roughly triangular in shape, instead of round. Such edge rolls are used for platform, padded, tight-tied spring, and spring-edge constructions as edge softeners, shapers, and stuffing retainers.

Stitched edge rolls for platform seats and backs. Cut a strip of burlap three times as wide as the desired roll height. Attach it to the platform as far back from the edge as the desired roll height. If the platform is solid, tack the strip using a tacking strip. Use parallel lengthwise threads in the strip as guides for cutting, tacking, or stitching. Pleat corners as described above for small rolls.

Use loose fiber filler such as hair, moss, or tow to stuff the roll. Remove any oversize pieces or foreign material from the stuffing fiber. Lay the burlap strip back on the platform and experiment to see how much filling is needed to produce the desired firmness and height when the burlap is pulled tightly over it and back down to the frame edge.

Working from the center of each side toward each corner, place the stuffing under the burlap strip, draw the string tautly over the stuffing, and tack it to the outer edge of the top of the rail or platform. Keep burlap smooth and shape the roll evenly as you proceed.

To achieve the roughly triangular cross-section shape, at least two rows of compression stitches will be placed parallel to the length of the roll. The rows

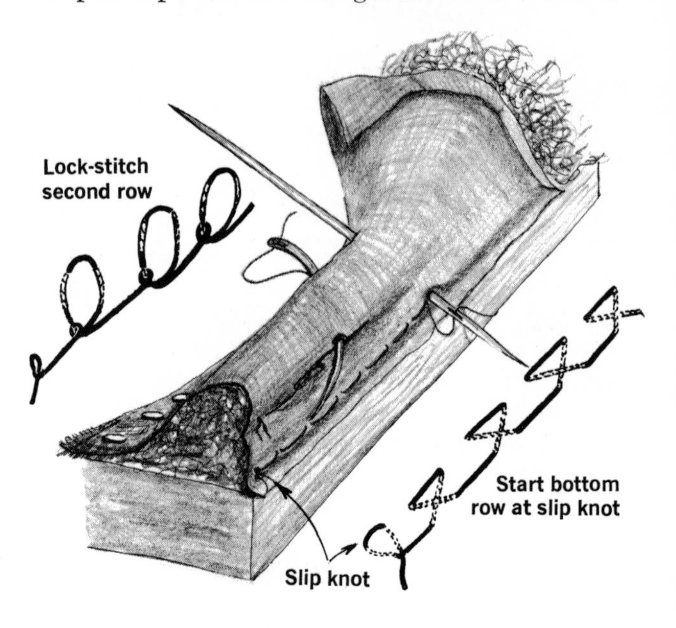

of stitches are merely overlapping loops used to compress the filling; the stitches in the first row are simple loops, and all subsequent rows of loops are lock-stitched in place.

Stitched edge rolls for spring-edge seats and backs. Stitched edge rolls for spring-edge construction are handled the same as stitched edge rolls for platform seats and backs except that the front edge of the burlap strip is stitched to the spring-covering burlap and edge wire. Use upholsterer's pins to fasten roll burlap to edge burlap and work out any irregularity before stitching. Use the same compression stitching methods shown on the opposite page for final shaping.

Stitched edge rolls for flat seats and backs. Cut strips of burlap equal in width to twice the distance from the frame tacking point to the top coil of the nearest spring.

Stitch one edge of the burlap roll strip to the burlap spring cover on a line ¾ to 1 inch back of the spring edges. Make pleats for corners as for small rolls (see page 25).

Place filling under the burlap strip, using tow for hard edges, hair or moss for medium-hard or soft edges. Draw the burlap strip down to the rail and slip-tack in position. Experiment with a 4-inch length to determine how much stuffing is needed for desired shape and firmness before proceeding. Start roll formation at edge centers and work to corners. By kneading and regulating, keep the roll smooth and even, uniform in thickness, and firm. When you are satisfied with the slip-tacked roll, remove slip tacks from a 4-inch length of roll at the center, make any final adjustments in shaping the roll, and turn the burlap edge up and tack through the doubled burlap to the seat rail. While tacking, keep the free edge of the burlap strip on top of the doubled burlap to absorb any possible tack-head cutting action.

Pinch and regulate the stuffing forward and up into a more triangular shape, then stitch by the same methods given for stitched edge rolls (page 26).

Stitched edge rolls for round seats. Round seats seldom require stitched edge rolls or rolls in excess of 1½ inches high. If one is required, use the method described above for flat seat stitched edge rolls but do not make the top of the roll as pointed or as high. In most cases commercial edge rolls can be used for round seats.

Cased understuffing

Arm and back understuffing held in shape by a tacked or stitched burlap case or cover is really a special type of edge roll. Spring backs which have exposed top rails or must be shaped to round or knife edges require a large edge roll shaped like the edge rolls used with flat seats. However, stitches through the stuffing may not be necessary if the roll is stuffed to a rounder, lower profile than for flat tied seats.

Back rails set below the tops of the back posts require a cased understuffing to bring the back to the height of the posts. (Any small edge rolls needed to shape or soften post edges should be added after the cased understuffing.) Cut a strip of burlap long enough to overlap both posts (allow for edge rolls if desired — see page 25) and 4 inches wider than the distance from the front of the rail up over the top of the posts to the back of the rail. Tack the burlap to the front of the rail. Place a layer of stuffing (approximately ¼ the desired uncovered thickness of the loose fibers) on the rail and tack in position to prevent slipping. Slip-tack the burlap to the front rail edge and partially over the top of the posts.

Place the remaining stuffing under the burlap to make a firm, well shaped roll. Tack the burlap to the back side of posts and rail. Make any necessary adjustments and drive the tacks in. Work out any lumps or voids in the stuffing.

Arm boards set below the tops of the arm stumps require almost the same cased understuffing treatment as low back rails. Often, however, the small edge rolls are installed before the understuffing stage —in fact, before the seat—since a completed seat could interfere with forming an edge roll along the seat-facing edge. If edge rolls are in place on the arm stump, it may be necessary to stitch the burlap to the edge roll instead of tacking it to the top of the stump. Turn the edge of the burlap under and stitch it to the roll. Be sure the stuffing is firm enough so that the roll is not pulled back from the edge.

If resilient second stuffing materials such as hair or moss are used for arm padding (see page 31) the cased understuffing can be built to the same height as the edge roll with a crowned center.

Since back posts and wings normally provide no top surface for arm-pad tacking, the burlap is tacked to a vertical surface. Trim the burlap to fit shape, fold the raw edge under, and tack the doubled thickness to the back post or wing. A way of avoiding this vertical tacking, which requires care to avoid wrinkles, is to add a thin tacking block to the vertical member. The block must be just thick enough to receive tacks and shaped to continue the arm shape. It must not be big enough to be noticeable visually or to the casual touch.

Stuffings and Muslin Covers

Stuffings provide padding over spring and frame edges, softening and shaping furniture lines. Ideally the stuffing gives enough resiliency so that upholstered surfaces and cushions return to shape after bearing weight. Both fiber and foam stuffings are used.

FIBER STUFFINGS

The best fiber stuffing is springy and has individual fibers long and tough enough to retain considerable curl. The closer the stuffing is to this ideal, the less it will pack down.

The most resilient fiber stuffing is hair, in either loose or rubberized form. Slab stock rubberized hair is best used for padding relatively straight lines of a piece of furniture, but where curves are involved loose hair is best. Moss, palm fiber, coco fiber, Tampico, sisal, wood wool excelsior, and tow follow hair in descending order of resiliency. For added comfort, finer-fibered, soft stuffings such as polyester, cotton felt, cotton felt substitutes, and kapok are used between the coarser, springier stuffings and the covers. Down and feathers are normally used for cushions only.

Coarse, resilient fiber stuffings

Hair from horses, cattle, or hogs is sorted, sterilized, and curled for the best fiber stuffing. The best loose fiber hair stuffing is made from horse and cattle hair. Hog hair is the least resilient as a loose fiber but is considerably upgraded when rubberized. The very best hair stuffing is made from long manes and tails of horses and cattle. The lower grades are varying mixtures of mane and tail hairs and short hog hair, hide scrapings, and vegetable fibers.

Rubberized hair and hair substitutes are available in pads of rubber bonded fibers and have a cloth reinforcing mesh bonded to the bottom side. Pads are readily available in ¾ or 1-inch thicknesses and also can be obtained in 2 and 2½-inch thicknesses. Lengths and widths vary among different manufacturers. Hair substitutes used include Tampico fibers and synthetics such as Saran. Tampico is usually identifiable by its golden or tan color, Saran by the multicolor fibers, and hair by its gray to black color. However, some manufacturers add sufficient color to the rubber bonding material so that fiber identification can be difficult. Rubberized fibers are used wherever slab stock is useful, but they make poor stuffings for complicated curves or shapes.

Moss is the processed fiber of the epiphytic plant that hangs in festoons from live oaks in the southern states and is known as Long, Louisiana, Southern, or Spanish moss. It ranks second to curled hair as a loose fiber stuffing, and the best quality is actually better than the lowest quality hairs. Moss is graded by the number of times it is processed. Dark brown moss, marked XXXX, is the best grade; green moss, marked XX, is the least resilient. Always fluff moss before using, and remove all stems and foreign particles.

Palm fiber is obtained from the leaves of several varieties of palms. Because of its low cost, ease of handling, cleanliness, and durability it is widely used as the only stuffing on inexpensive grades of furniture. On better grades it is used only as a bulk space filler or spring insulator (to eliminate the feel of the separate springs) under more resilient stuffings such as foam, hair, or moss.

Coco fiber is the coarse brown fiber on the coconut shell. It ranks high in cleanliness, durability, and strength but very low in resiliency and ease of handling. It packs down into matlike layers which make it primarily useful as a spring insulator.

Tampico fiber is obtained from various species of Mexican agave plants. It looks like a shorter-fibered sisal and is fairly resilient, clean, durable, and easy to handle. It is best used as a spring insulator, as a bulk understuffing beneath hair, moss, or foam, or in the form of rubberized slabs as second stuffing.

Sisal fiber, produced from the leaves of the sisal plant, provides a clean, durable, easy-to-handle material for non-resilient understuffing or spring insulation required for a hard or firm shape. The creamy white fiber is sold both loose and as felted mats.

Excelsior is a shredded wood product familiar as a packing material. Poor resiliency and rapid matting limit it to use as an insulator. A high grade version called wood wool is sometimes found in hard, stitched edge rolls. Its characteristic of breaking up into sawdustlike particles leads to rapid breakdown of shapes and dirty handling.

Tow is the clean, easy-to-handle, non-resilient, long fiber produced from the stalks of the flax plant. Its characteristics of matting and packing into hard layers make it ideal for use in spring insulation or the construction of edge rolls. It is often hard to find from local sources without special order.

Soft, fine-fibered stuffings

Cotton felt ranges from tough, resilient, and soft long-fibered staple fiber to short-fibered linters. Long-fibered staple is the result of the first processing of material removed from cotton bolls. Linters is a short-fibered, cotton gin by-product cut from cotton seed and felted into sheets; it makes a weaker, less resilient, lumpier padding. The higher the staple fiber content is, the less the material weighs by the yard and the more resilient it is. Unfortunately, good staple cotton felt is becoming hard to find.

Cotton felt substitutes are available in a number of manmade or processed materials ranging from polyester mats and quilted batts to resilient bonded wood fiber sheets. Paper and paper-cotton-linters felts should be avoided because of their low resiliency and rapid breakdown.

Down and feathers for upholstery are obtained from water fowl. Down is the quill-less, extremely soft, light, and warm material that covers newly hatched birds and underlies the feathers of grown birds; it is especially plentiful on geese and ducks. Without equal among natural fibers for warmth, softness, lightness, and compressability, it is ideal for sleeping bags and quilts. Except for extremely slack-filled shapeless effects, down is never used as a furniture stuffing without at least 20 per cent (by volume) goose or duck feather fill. For this mixture goose feathers are the best because they have curved, springy quills with more fluffy fibers than any other commercially available feather. Duck feathers share the desirable qualities of goose feathers but to a lesser degree. Chicken and turkey feathers should be avoided as they are stiff and brittle and tend to pack down. Fluffed fibers stripped from the quills of chicken and turkey feathers are sometimes used as adulterants for down. It is a good idea to check down for presence of these fibers.

CLEAN loose fiber by picking it apart; felt it by overlapping and working together small amounts.

Polyester fibers have become increasingly popular wherever a downlike, non-allergenic stuffing is required. Polyester is soft, clean, and durable, and it holds its shape much better than down. It is widely used between foam and pillow casings to give a soft, unstretched cover a puffy look.

Kapok, sometimes called silk cotton, silk floss, or tree silk, occurs as a silky fiber that cushions the seeds within the pods of the kapok tree *(Ceiba pentandra)*. The fiber does not absorb moisture and is therefore often used to stuff boat cushions, mattresses, and life preservers. A relatively resilient stuffing initially, it packs down under continuous pressure, separating, lumping, and breaking up into powdery particles.

Preparing fiber stuffing for use

Both new and used fiber stuffing should be picked apart to break up hard-packed portions, then fluffed up; any foreign or oversized particles should be removed. You may be able to find an upholsterer who will run your fibers through his picking machine. To hand-pick fibers, take a small amount in one hand and pinch or pick off small pieces with the other. Continue until all the fiber is thoroughly fluffed and cleaned. Wear gloves to protect your skin while working with large quantities of coarse and prickly materials used for second stuffings.

Salvage any stuffing which can be cleaned, fluffed,

or reworked and handled easily—especially costly materials such as down or materials that are hard to purchase locally. Cotton felt, palm fiber, coco, excelsior, kapok, sisal, and loose Tampico fibers can be reused but are cheap enough that new material is more practical; always use a fresh layer of cotton felt over old cotton.

Three stuffing layers

In the following discussion fiber stuffings will be divided into three layers: first stuffings, second stuffings, and top paddings. First stuffings—often called understuffings—provide cushioning which hides the feel of spring and frame irregularities, fill in voids, and provide basic shapes to support more resilient stuffing. Materials used may include any of the coarser fibers. Cost usually dictates the use of the less expensive materials for the first stuffing, leaving the more costly materials for second stuffing and top padding.

First stuffings or understuffings are always tacked, stitched, glued, or burlap-cased to the supporting surface materials to prevent shifting. Second stuffings are the layers which supply the major stuffing resiliency and make use of hair, moss, rubberized fiber, or foam. Top paddings are made of the softest, smoothest materials available (such as cotton felt, polyester batting, or loose fiber) to provide a smooth surface for the cover material and cushion any minor irregularities in the lower stuffing, especially prickly strands of hair.

On many commercial pieces you will find non-resilient stuffings used as both first and second stuffing directly under a thin layer of cotton felt. This is less expensive but also less comfortable than using resilient second stuffing. The very finest pieces often have high-quality resilient stuffing materials—hair, moss, foam, or rubberized hair for both first and second stuffings. In some cases, because of the nature of the surface, first or first and second stuffings may be omitted and only a top stuffing used, as on simple pad seats or outer surfaces of chairs and couches.

First stuffings. Ideally, the very finest, most resilient stuffing such as hair or moss should be used throughout a piece of furniture, but the high cost of the better stuffings prevents this for most projects. Where springs, uneven supports, or awkward frame shapes necessitate filling out, shaping, insulating, or leveling, less expensive fibers will do the job. In fact, for spring insulation the longer-fibered materials such as sisal, tow, palm, and Tampico provide better leveling for less work since they pack down into compact mats.

Edge rolls (see page 24) act as retainers along frame edges for first stuffings and with few exceptions establish the limit of the edge thickness. First stuffings are usually made level with the edge roll. Where non-resilient, hard-packing materials are used, a hollowed first stuffing profile is sometimes used to ensure an extra thickness of the more springy top stuffing in the center, especially for seats. In general, use enough non-resilient or matted first stuffing to cushion spring or base irregularities but as little as the higher cost of second stuffing will permit. Rubberized fiber can be used for both first and second stuffing wherever its slab form can be utilized.

After the fiber is picked and fluffed, take a handful and distribute it in a thin, even layer over the surface to be stuffed. Each pinch of material should slightly overlap and be pressed or worked into the last. Build up the first stuffing, layer upon thin layer, until the desired contour is achieved and the fiber reaches the level of the edge roll or slightly overlaps it. Correct hard and soft, high and low spots as you work.

If the stuffing is over a solid base, tack the first stuffing layer to the base by making small openings in the fiber to about three quarters its depth, then tacking through the remaining depth. If stuffing is applied directly over burlapped webbing or springs, stitch it to the burlap by using a double pointed upholsterer's needle and stitching twine. Make a line of stitches, either spiralling in from a corner or outward from the center. Start with a very short stitch and tie with a slip knot (see next page), catching a little stuffing to avoid forming a hard lump under the knot. Stitch the stuffing to the burlap with 2 to 3-inch stitches running over the stuffing but ⅜-inch—never more than ¾-inch—stitches under the burlap.

Stitch in spiral pattern conforming to seat shape

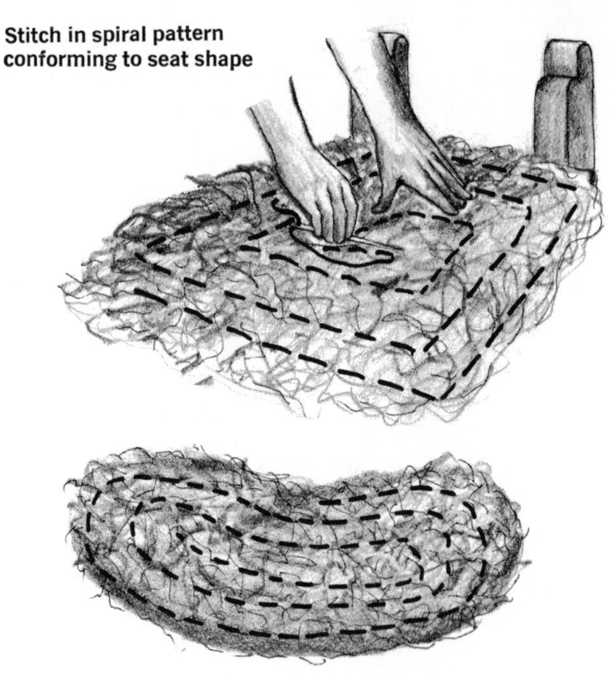

Spring-seat first stuffing is done by the same rules that apply to stuffing over webbing. Round-seat first

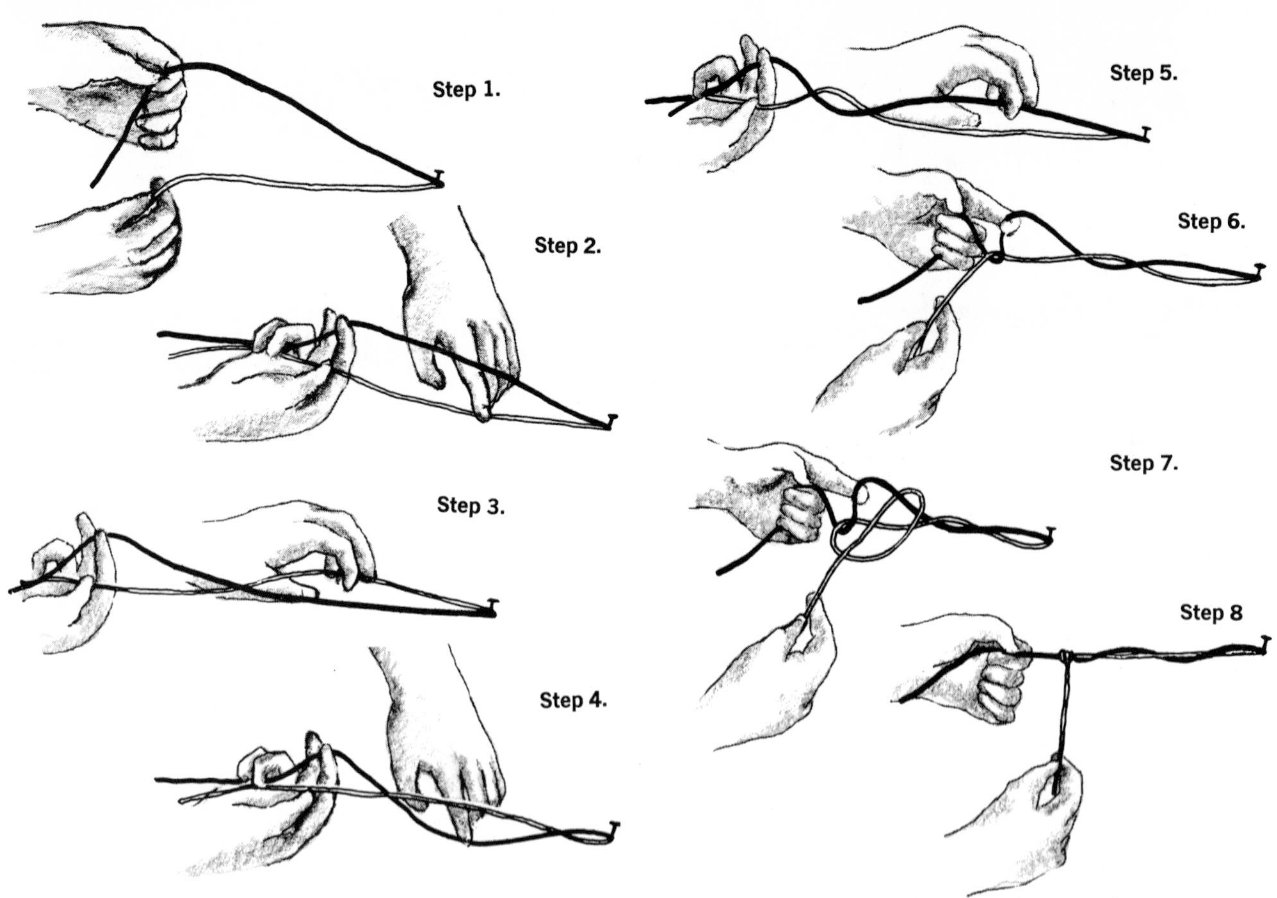

SLIP KNOTS, often used in furniture upholstery, can be tied quickly by the steps illustrated here. Both string ends are held in the right hand for Steps 2 through 5 while the left hand makes two half twists. Hold the left-hand (dark) twine taut after Step eight or the knot may jam.

stuffings are still limited by the height of the edge rolls. Though the seat is raised in the center, an even thickness of first stuffing is distributed up and over the rounded seat crown. It may be necessary to insert extra stuffing material in the depression between the edge rolls and springs and to stitch it to the spring cover before placing stuffing over the crown of the seat.

Flat, platform, and spring-edge seats are limited in first stuffing thickness by the roll edges at their free edges and are tapered in the last 1 to 1½ inches at edges against stuffed arms or backs.

Back first stuffing can be handled exactly as seat first stuffing except that the rounded spring-edge rolls (often called cased understuffings on backs) may not supply a raised retaining lip for the stuffing as the seat edges do. Stuffing thickness is determined by the edge rolls on the frame edges.

Arms are seldom designed to have the deep padding used on seats and backs. With the exception of barrel-back and similar chairs and couches which have the insides of the arms sprung or padded like backs, the insides and outsides of arms have a thin layer of top stuffing largely for shape and appearance. If the arm board is flush with the top of the arm stump, complete stuffing depth is governed by the ½ to ¾-inch edge roll diameter, and the arm is handled like a pad seat. Softer arms are formed where cased understuffing is used to build up an armboard to arm stump height. On square arms, rubberized fiber slabs are an ideal replacement for cased understuffing. Slab fiber stock can be used for both first and second stuffing.

Wing stuffing should be done at the same time as the arms to which they are attached. If wings are obviously part of the back and not the arm structure, stuffing should be done at the time of back stuffing. Stuffing often consists only of a layer or two of cotton felt. Where deeper stuffing is required, use the same techniques as for pad seats.

Second stuffings. The stuffing materials which provide most of the resiliency are the hair, moss, rubberized fiber, or foams used as second stuffings. In furniture requiring maximum comfort and quality, they make up the bulk of the material. If foam is used, it may serve as first and second stuffing and top padding. In a few cases—such as platform seats with loose cushions—resilient second stuffings are not needed between first stuffing and top padding.

Uncompressed hair or moss will have to be built up to a free-standing height two or three times its

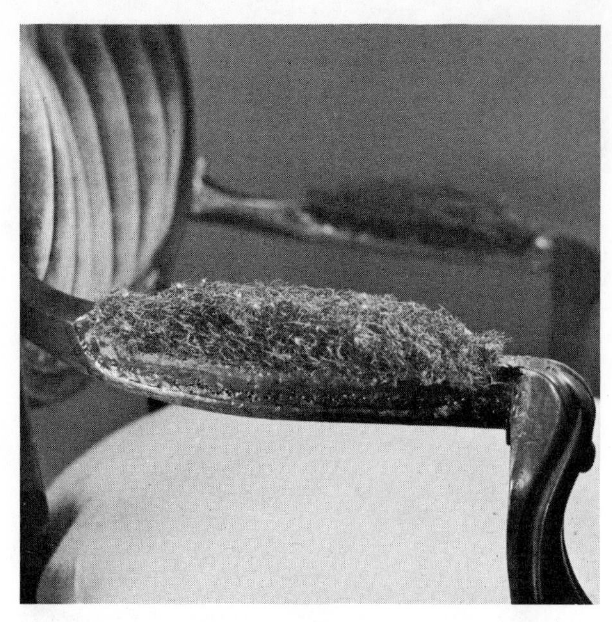

CROWN STUFFINGS to compensate for tendency of covers to pull at edges. Degree depends on style.

FELTED COTTON padding is often used directly over second stuffings but can instead be used over muslin.

desired compressed height before adequate density is achieved. Check by applying pressure with the palm of your hand. If you can feel the first stuffing, webbing, or springs, more second stuffing is needed.

Crown all second stuffings (except on sag seats) to compensate for the difference in compression produced by the fastening or pulling of covers to or around edges. Covers applied over perfectly flat second stuffings soon develop sagged centers. Build the centers up to a gentle mound, according to the size and shape you desire in the finished piece.

Build the second stuffing layer on layer in the same way described for first stuffings. If loose fiber second stuffing is to be applied over cased understuffings or severely curved first stuffing shapes, it is a good idea to use stitching twine and a curved needle to loosely stitch the two together to prevent the stuffing from slipping. A muslin casing is often used over second stuffings in addition to stitching or in place of it to compress the fibers to their final shape. Any shaping and stuffing errors are far easier to correct at this stage than after the final cover is on. See page 35 for a discussion of muslin covers.

Top paddings. The silky-soft top padding material smooths out any remaining harshness, small bumps, or voids in the lower stuffings and prevents coarse, sharp fibers from penetrating the cover. The most commonly used material is felted cotton, followed by foam, cotton felt substitutes, polyester fiber, and occasionally rayon and kapok fibers. Top paddings are sometimes used alone for places where thin, uniform, appearance-only padding is desired (inside and outside of arms and outside of backs) and for pad seats. Crowned top padding is produced by laying concentric layers of padding on top of each other with the smallest on the bottom, so that the largest is on top to present a smooth face to the cover.

Over other stuffings, use one or more layers of cotton, synthetic felt, or polyester fiber for the top padding.

Top padding should overhang small edge rolls slightly on pad or round and flat tight-spring seats or backs. Spring-edge seats call for filling the space between the base of the spring-edge roll and the rail with a layer or two of top padding to level the exposed face, then placing a continuous layer of padding over the entire stuffed seat from the back, over the spring-edge rolls, to the bottom of the front rail if an unbroken seat front is desired or to the top of the rail if a stuffed border (see page 52) will be used.

Platform seats for loose cushions need only a single layer of cotton top padding over a thin, spring-insulating first stuffing, since the platform itself is not required to be comfortable for sitting. The padding is laid down in two major sections after the muslin (or the cover and platform decking where a muslin is not used) has been sewn along the back edge of the spring edge. Refer to page 35 for details about muslin covers.

FOAM STUFFINGS

Foam rubber or polyurethane are in many ways ideal stuffing materials for the amateur upholsterer to work with, since they don't require the meticulous felting that fiber materials need to obtain maximum resiliency and even density.

Foam rubber is latex whipped to a froth and solidified with millions of interconnected air cells enmeshed between webs of rubber. The interconnection of the air cells provides a self cleansing and cooling "pump" or "breathing" action when foam is compressed. This air-passing property is also used in air filters made of polyurethane and related synthetic foams for painters' masks, auto air filters, and air conditioners. (It should be noted that there is a great difference between foam and sponge rubber. Sponge rubber has bubbles that have been encapsulated in the rubber with no interconnection between bubbles.)

Foam densities are designated as extra soft, soft, medium, firm, and extra firm. Not all foams are available from every manufacturer in all densities. The same designations apply roughly to rubberized fibers. Density is controlled by the relative space occupied by solids and air. The harder or firmer the density, the more solids per given volume and therefore the heavier the foam.

Surfaces that require little smoothing or cushioning, such as solid or webbed seats or solid arm tops, very often need only a slab of solid or pin-cored foam stock to provide all three stuffing layers in one operation. Better padding is obtained if the foam slab is built up in two or three layers of different densities. Most commonly a layer of firm density is used under a layer of soft density. Less common, but very effective, is the use of three layers—firm, medium, and very soft. Polyester or cotton felt top padding is becoming increasingly popular over foam to create less of an "elastic band" tautness to the final fabric cover.

The uneven surfaces of coil or zig-zag springs, or surfaces that need building up or filling, such as arm tops recessed between back post and arm stumps, require that first stuffings of fiber materials be used for cushioning and shaping. The foam stock can then be used over the fiber stuffing as both second stuffing and top padding or as second stuffing under a cotton or polyester top padding.

Thin layers of foam are often used as top padding over first and second stuffings in automobile upholstery and some adequate but not comfortable furniture. Rubberized hair slab is often used as a combination first and second stuffing for this type of construction.

Tools and materials

A serrated-edge bread knife or, better yet, an electric carving knife is the only special tool needed when working with foam stuffing. A wood-cutting band saw or a common foam cutter simplifies foam cutting considerably but isn't really practical unless extensive use can justify the high initial price.

Special materials for working with foam include talc powder, anti-sticking compound, foam adhesive, and tacking tape. Talc is used to absorb excess adhesive and to reduce tackiness of foam surfaces; any good, unscented talc dusting powder can be used if your local dealer doesn't carry the cruder commercial variety. Where a powdery residue would be objectionable, spray-type slip or anti-stick compounds can be used to reduce friction.

Foam adhesives should be matched to the particular foam and manufacturer for best results. They must provide joints that remain as soft as the surrounding foam. Cheap or mismatched adhesives often give hard joint lines that become brittle and crumble. Both spray and liquid adhesives are available. Though higher in cost, the spray cans are simpler to use. Keep a small container of the recommended kind of adhesive solvent in which to clean and store the spray can nozzle when not in use; follow instructions on the solvent container.

Tacking tape is cloth tape used to hold foam in position. It is available in several widths from 2 to 6 inches, with either full surface adhesive or a 1-inch strip of adhesive along one edge. Muslin can be cut to width, coated with foam adhesive, and dried for use as a tacking tape substitute.

Preparing the supporting surface

Preparation of surfaces to receive foam stuffing is especially important. Solid surfaces must have sufficient air vents to allow rapid, noise-free compression and spring-back of the foam. (See page 7 for details on venting frames under foam.) This is even more critical if the cover material is airtight, such as leather or plastic. Perforated sheet metal or metal grid may be used over cutouts in solid surfaces for a vented foam support instead of ordinary vent holes.

Supporting surfaces must be free of sharp curves, lumps, or voids. Any uneven places must be built up with fiber understuffings to provide a relatively smooth surface. Loose fiber stuffings should be encased in burlap so that the foam can be cemented to the burlap. Fiber mats or rubberized fibers need not be burlap-covered if they will accept foam cement.

Webbed supporting surfaces should have at least ½-inch air spaces between webs. Though not absolutely necessary, a layer of taut burlap stitched on top of the webs helps provide a good cementing surface.

Springs must be insulated before foam is installed. Use sisal or rubberized fiber mats stitched to the burlap spring covers before foam is installed. Some commercial pieces simply have a heavier-than-normal burlap over the springs, especially on zig-zag springs, and the foam is cemented to the burlap. This is a time saver, but for the do-it-yourself upholsterer any time saved isn't worth the shortened life of the foam.

Edge rolls are not needed to retain foam stuffing on most flat surfaces as they are for loose stuffing, but they may still be necessary if irregular surfaces must be built up with loose fiber understuffings. Foam-stuffed spring-edge seats do not require spring-edge rolls, but platform seats do. An interesting variation on the spring-edge roll can be made by cementing a wedge-shaped slab of extra firm foam to the burlap at the spring edge. Allow a ½-inch overhang beyond the edge wire for upholstery or compression allowance. Cover the foam wedge with taut burlap exactly as for a standard spring edge (see page 23), but shaping stitches will not be necessary.

Cutting and cementing the foam

Cutting foam is relatively easy as long as you take into account three characteristics of foam—it tries to move with the cutting tool, it bulges and compresses under cutting tools, and it has a built-in tackiness that "grabs" tools. Never try to cut all the way through foam that is more than 2 inches thick with anything other than a band saw, a commercial foam cutter, or an electric carving knife. To cut foam with a sharp razor blade or serrated bread knife, draw the blade gently but firmly across it, attempting a 1-inch-deep cut or 2 inches at the most. To attempt a deeper cut compresses the foam so much that even though the blade is kept vertical, the cut edge of the foam may be slanted. Repeat the shallow cuts until the entire thickness is separated. A similar series of shallow cuts is also advisable if you use scissors. Lubricate the scissors with a silicone dry lubricant spray or water when cutting form slabs.

Bevels and curves should be cut with as much care as straight cuts. Scissors usually do a better job than a knife. Cut in gradual stages, increasing the amount of curve until the correct shape is achieved. Rough edges can be buffed smooth with either a power disc or belt sander or a hand sanding block with numbers 80 or 120 aluminum oxide or garnet paper.

Cementing foam rubber is a simple process. When using commercial tacking tape, apply adhesive to the foam only. Allow to become tacky, then position and press on the dry adhesive strip of the tacking tape. If preglued tacking tape is not used, always apply adhesive to both surfaces to be joined, whether foam to foam or base to foam. Allow to dry to tacky stage, gently position, then press surfaces together. Once pressed together, the surfaces are very difficult to separate, so correct positioning is important.

Normal handling is possible within ten minutes after applying most adhesives, but don't apply heavy stress to foam-to-foam joints for several hours after cementing; solvents in the glue can soften the foam enough for its shape to be permanently changed under severe pressure or pull. Foam-to-wood, metal, or fabric cemented joints should set several hours before handling, since these joints invariably receive considerable stress.

Dust all surfaces near the joint with talc to absorb excess adhesive; if cored stock is used, be sure to dust talc into core holes to prevent collapse caused by cementing cores shut.

Add an upholstery allowance of ¼ inch for each 6 inches of length for medium density foam, more for soft density, less for firm density.

Crowned foam pads

You can make crowned foam pads either by using a piece of foam as thick as the desired crown and then cutting down the edges or by using foam as thick as the edge height and building up the center with additional foam slabs.

If you start with a foam slab the same thickness as the desired crown height, cut the slab to the desired shape (add upholstery allowance to each dimension) and lay it upside down. For a front-to-back crown only, mark a line across the front and back faces of the slab indicating the desired edge thickness measured up from the work surface (actually the eventual top surface of the foam). Draw lines on the adjoining sides indicating the actual crown shape desired; these lines should not meet in the center but should intersect the surface 4 to 6 inches from the edge. Cut away all foam below the lines (small cuts are easier to control than one big cut) and buff smooth if necessary.

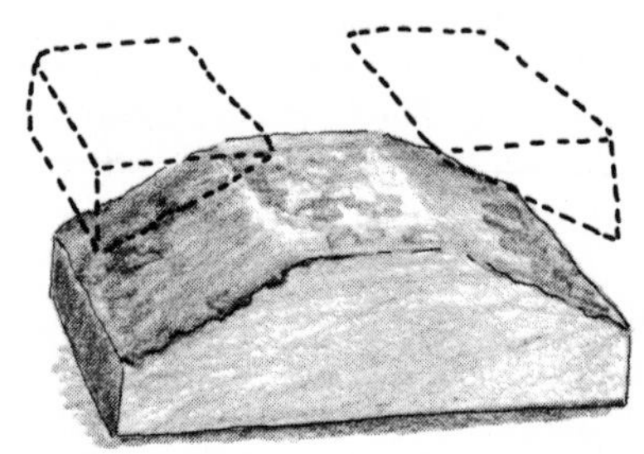

Cut away foam to form crown

If the piece is to be crowned from all sides, mark edge height on all sides and then draw lines 4 to 6 inches in from and parallel to the edges on the face-up bottom surface of the foam. Cut from these lines to the edge-height lines on the sides. When the crown contour is to be curved, a cardboard template cut to crown shape will be very helpful in keeping a constant shape while cutting away the waste. Turn the cut slab over. The edges will be raised off the surface. Press the edges down until they touch the supporting surface. If there is too much of a taper on the crowned edges, it may be necessary to trim them back to vertical and cement on a thin foam strip to restore upholstery allowance.

The second method of making a crowned foam pad starts with a slab the same thickness as the desired edge height. Determine the difference between edge and crown height and choose additional thin slab stock half that thick to use for the crown. If edge height is 3 inches and crown height is 5 inches, the crowning slabs should be 1 inch thick. Cut the first of the thin crowning slabs so that its edges fall 2 to 3 inches back from each edge that is to be crowned, but flush to each uncrowned edge. Cement it in place in the center of the bottom of the primary slab. Cut the second of the thin crowning slabs so that its edges are 2 to 3 inches back from the edges of the previously cut crowning slab at all crowned edges (this distance should be exactly the same as the distance from the edge to the first crowning slab), and flush to the primary slab on the uncrowned edges. Cement in place. With small slabs face down, press the outside edges of the foam assembly down to the supporting surface. If the edges of the crowning slabs cause ridges that are visible or uncomfortable, bevel them. Cement the foam to the supporting surface.

Tacking tape should be used on the edges of crowned foam to help hold them down. Use the method described in the following section for shaping square edges.

Shaping the edges

Round edges can be formed with the help of tacking tape. Cut the foam large enough so that it overhangs the supporting surface. A ¼-inch overhang is about right for a 1-inch thickness, ½-inch overhang for a 2-inch thickness, ¾-inch for a 3 to 4-inch thickness, and 1-inch for a 5 to 6-inch thickness. Cement an inch of the tacking tape to the top of the foam edge to be rounded. Pull down on the free edge of the tacking tape at a 45-degree angle with one hand. With the other hand, fold under the bottom edge of the foam, then pull the taped top foam edge to the supporting surface and tack or stitch the tape to the support.

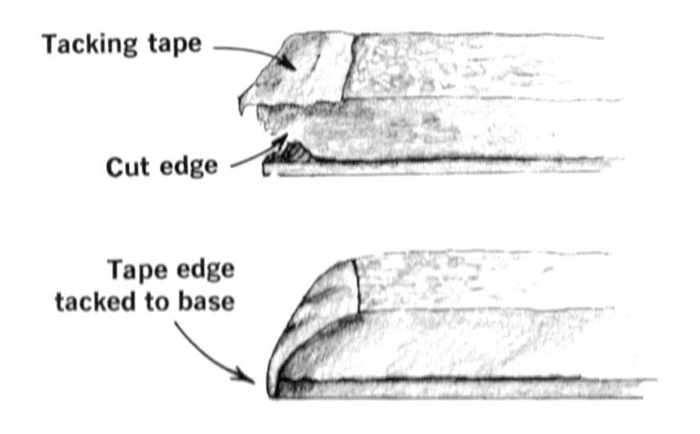

Contoured or feathered edges are simply variations on the round edge, with gentler curves obtained by cutting the overhanging edges to taper inward. The greater the angle of taper is, the gentler the edge curve will be. Cement the tacking tape to the top foam edge before cutting the taper, then gradually cut back the vertical face until the desired shape is obtained when the edge is folded under and the tacking tape pulled down to the supporting surface. Fasten the tape to this surface as for round seats.

Straight edges are made by cutting slab stock to the desired size and shape, leaving standard upholstery allowances on each edge. Make all cuts at right angles to the top surface. Cement tacking tape to the entire edge surface and tack or stitch the free tape edge to the supporting member.

MUSLIN COVERS FOR STUFFING

Use of muslin covers over stuffing has declined considerably in recent years on commercial pieces because of the time required to install them. However, the finest pieces still have muslin under the final fabric cover. The muslin compresses the stuffing to the desired density and shape and takes most of the stuffing pressure off the outer cover. It also provides a "practice round" at installing covers—especially useful to the beginning upholsterer.

Unbleached muslin is the material normally used, though any material of similar weight, weave, and strength may be used. Avoid thin, bedsheet-type bleached muslins or heavy, canvaslike materials. The first is too weak and the latter too stiff for easy handling.

You can use muslin either between the second stuffing and the top padding or between the top padding and the outer cover. When only foam is used as stuffing or as top padding and the outer cover will be a piled cloth such as velvet, muslin is used over the top padding to keep the foam from rubbing against the underside of the velvet and pulling its pile through the fabric. Muslin also is used over the top padding if foam is used under weak or delicate outer fabrics, such as thin silks. Another situation requiring muslin over top padding is when the cover fabric is so finely woven, light in color, or glossy that any attempt to insert a regulator through it to adjust stuffing would leave a mark.

Except for color, texture, and final edge trim, muslin over top padding lets you see exactly how the outer cover will look. Defects in stuffing, such as hollows, lumps, sags, and poor shaping of corners, all show up under the plain muslin wrapper in time for correction. If a mistake is found, a muslin undercover is much cheaper to replace than the final cover. With inexpensive muslin in place over all stuffing and top padding, you can make accurate measurements that enable you to cut the expensive outer cover with the least possible waste material.

Muslin placed under top padding has a few definite advantages. It holds the coarser first and second stuffings in place, and it compresses the first and second stuffing to final height and density, making it fairly easy to detect voids, lumps, or shaping defects. Stuffing can be regulated through muslin, when it may not be possible through final covers. Finally, the outer surface may feel softer without a taut muslin surface directly reinforcing the final cover, especially if the finest quality long staple cotton felt or polyester is used as top padding.

Attaching the muslin

To determine muslin size, decide where the muslin will be tacked on the frame, then place a tape measure across the stuffing between opposite tacking points (front and back rails, top rail and back liner, or arm board and arm liner), pull the stuffing down to final height, and measure. Add 4 inches to each dimension for ease in handling.

Slip-tack the muslin to the center points of the back, front, and sides. If there are arm or back posts or other interfering members, mark and cut the muslin as described for burlap, page 23. Keep the muslin taut and wrinkle-free as you compress the stuffing and slip-tack toward all corners from the centerline tacks. Drive a slip tack or two each side of the center tack on one rail, then do the same on the opposite rail and the adjoining rails; continue until you reach the corners. It is much easier to work the muslin free of wrinkles this way than if you complete one side at a time. For both muslin and outer covers, a good way to keep the cover smooth as you proceed with tacking is to grasp the fabric 2 to 3 inches from the last tack, pull taut and wrinkle-free, then drive a tack halfway between the grip point and the last tack. When pull marks—wrinkles beginning at tack heads—occur, simply remove the slip tack, adjust the fabric, and retack. An alternative often used for slight pull marks is to make a slight slit in the fabric under the tack head, just long enough to release tension. However, with this technique there is the danger that too large a cut may be made or the slit might become a rip under the pressure of use.

Corners should be neatly pleated. A single butterfly pleat should be used for square corners and a series of small flat pleats for round corners.

Strong cross light is best for checking the slip-tacked muslin for pull marks, hollows, wrinkles, or other faults. A small workshop trouble light is easy to move around to provide strong cross light from many angles. Repair any defects by removing the necessary slip tacks, adjusting the muslin, then slip-tacking again. Drive slip tacks home only when all adjustments have been made. Some stuffing adjustments will still be possible by using a regulator through the muslin (see page 37), but it is best to produce a perfect surface before driving in the slip tacks.

Muslin covers for spring-edge seats

Muslin covers for spring-edge platform seats are handled differently than for other types of seats. The muslin is temporarily stretched directly over the first stuffing or spring insulator, and then cotton felt is inserted between the first stuffing and muslin before the muslin is permanently attached.

SINGLE BUTTERFLY PLEAT gives right-angled corners a neat, crisp line; stitch the pleat shut at the corner. On curves, several small pleats should be used instead of a single pleat.

On platforms with a single spring-edge roll on the front of the seat, slip-tack the muslin to each rail, working from the center of each rail, then stitch it to the back edge of the stitched spring-edge roll. Remove the slip tacks from back and side rails and bring the back part of the muslin forward. Then fit a sheet of cotton felt flush with the line of sewing and underlapping the back and arm liners. Pull the muslin back over the cotton pad, slip-tack it at the center of the back rail, and proceed to slip-tack, adjust, then tack the muslin along the entire back rail. When this tacking is complete, remove the slip tacks controlling the front half of the muslin. Lay the muslin back over the completed back portion, and place a sheet of cotton felt flush with the line of stitching and extending over the stitched spring edge to either the spring-edge wire, the top of the rail, or the bottom of the rail, depending on the visual effect desired from the front. Draw the loose muslin forward over the cotton felt. If the felt ends at the wire edge, tack it to the wire with upholsterer's pins or skewers; otherwise tack it to the rail. Start at the center and work to the ends, keeping the muslin smooth. Then stitch the muslin to the burlap at the spring edge wire. Fit sufficient layers of cotton felt between the spring edge and rail to provide a flat stuffed surface. Pull the loose muslin taut from the spring edge to the rail, then slip-tack. Correct any pull marks, then drive home all slip tacks. Make corner pleats as flat and smooth as possible; the simple butterfly pleat is good for sharp corners, and series of small, close-fitting pleats may be necessary to round more gradual corners.

Platforms with more than one spring edge call for a slight variation in covers to allow for the corners where spring-edge rolls join each other. Proceed as for the single spring edge, but stitch the muslin along the whole length of the back edge of the front spring-edge roll. Do not at this time continue stitching across or along the back edge of joining spring-edge rolls. Bring the back part of the muslin forward. Fit a layer of cotton felt flush with the rear edges of all spring-edge rolls, underlapping back and arm liners. Draw the muslin back over the cotton felt, stretch it taut, slip-tack at center lines, then slip-tack toward each corner. Stitch the muslin along the back edges of the side spring-edge rolls. You will need to remove slip tacks along the edge being stitched in order to get a smooth, pull-free stitching job.

With stitching complete, lay the outer edge strips of the muslin back over the decking, then fit strips of cotton felt over the spring edges as for single spring-edge platforms but with a mitered tear made in the felt so corners will be smooth. Pull the muslin forward over the cotton felt and continue as for the single spring edge cover. Take particular care with the butterfly pleats at the corners, since they will be more noticeable at spring-edge corners.

STUFFING RODS AND STUFFING REGULATORS

Stuffing rods and regulators are two tools you can use to make stuffing adjustments. Stuffing rods are steel bars used to push stuffing into difficult-to-reach spaces, and regulators are sharp, tapered steel needles that can be used even after the muslin cover—and sometimes the final cover—is in place.

Stuffing rods have one or both ends flattened; one end often has a gently serrated tip, and the other may have a hole. Smooth wooden strips 1 to 1½ inches wide, ⅛-inch thick, and 24 to 36 inches long can be substituted for steel stuffing rods. A hardwood yardstick is ideal.

To use a stuffing rod to push felted stuffing into cushions, lap the felt over the end of the rod, position it in the cushion, and work the lapped section flat with the end of the rod. To work rolled felted cotton into channels, attach a 1 to 2-inch by 24-inch strip of muslin, denim, or tape to one end of the rod. Place the rolled felt on the rod and hold it flat by pulling the attached strip tightly over the felt along the rod. Push the rod, belted end first, into the sewn channel until the tip shows through the other end. Release your hold on the strip, pull it through from the bottom of the channel, and withdraw the rod.

There are two kinds of stuffing regulators. The traditional English pattern regulator has a flattened end, and others have blunt ends and look something like ice picks. Of the two types, English pattern regulators are the more useful.

The flat end of a regulator is used as a miniature stuffing rod to push or prod materials into place or to slide between layers to smooth them out. The flat end can be threaded with twine to use where a sharp needle might cause cover damage. The sharp end is used to pierce muslin casing and some outer covers in order to move stuffing without having to remove the casing. Insert the point through the casing material a little to one side of the midpoint between the stuffing and the place to which it is to be moved. Slide the regulator point into the stuffing and work the stuffing into place. On cover fabrics, cradle the entry point between thumb and forefinger to prevent cover damage.

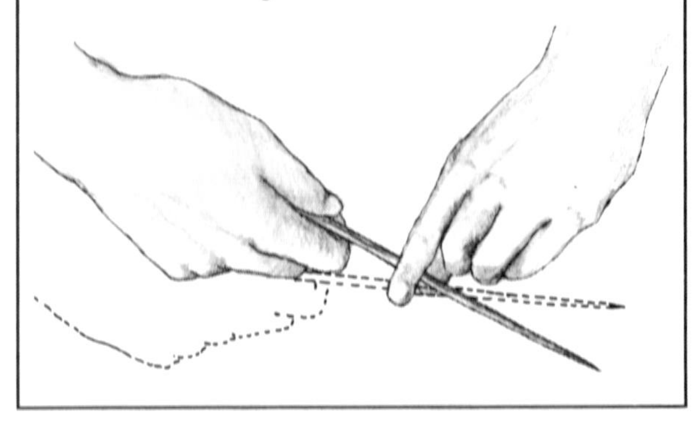

Channeling and Tufting

Two upholstery procedures that are used to vary the appearance of furniture surfaces are channeling and tufting. Both are utilitarian as well as decorative, in that they make outer covers conform to curved inner surfaces such as those on barrel-back chairs.

Commercial production of channeled and tufted pieces in the low to medium price ranges has gradually decreased, as both procedures are time consuming. However, you can make channeled and tufted furniture yourself. For best results, choose cover materials that have no pattern, unless you can find a pattern that will fall evenly in channel or tuft divisions.

CHANNELING

Also called piping, fluting, and shell backing, channeling is the process of enclosing stuffing in fabric pipes or channels to give an essentially vertical ribbed effect. On some pieces channels may spread out to fill fan or shell backs or other special shapes, in which case the channels are usually wider at the top end. Occasionally a modern variation has horizontally aligned, thick, foam-filled channels used as body-conforming, free-hanging seat and back panels on lounging chairs.

Channel widths range from 1 to 8 inches. Narrow channels give the appearance of slenderness, height, and depth. Wide channels tend to make furniture look less formal, wider, and less deeply padded. The width of channel to be used depends largely on the period and style of the piece and the preference of the upholsterer. Unless you are duplicating the original channeling on a chair, the number and placement of channels is pretty much up to you. More important is that channels be relatively uniform in size, shape, and width and that all be stuffed to the same density. When outer channels lap over the outside frame, their width should be the same as the center channels, unless some special effect is desired.

Supporting surfaces for channeling should be prepared exactly as for normal stuffing, though edge rolls are seldom used except to provide a recess for post or arm stump panels (see page 53). Use cased understuffing to fill in scroll backs, round arms, or other shape voids that would normally be built up. Channeling must be over burlap-cased stuffing, never loose stuffing. On a tied-spring barrel back, arrange the channels so that the depressions between them fall on the springs; this ensures better support, shaping, and sewing surface. Using burlap to provide channel support between springs on barrel backs will not work, since the burlap would interfere with spring action.

Decide how many channels will be used. An even number of channels will place a depression on the center of the surface being covered; an odd number will center a channel on the centerline. To find the top width of each channel, divide the distance across the top of the surface to be channeled by the number of channels. To find the bottom width of each channel, divide the distance across the bottom of the surface to be channeled by the number of channels. If a modified fan back 31½ inches across the top and 21 inches across the bottom is to have seven channels, they would be 4½ inches wide at the top and 3 inches wide at the bottom. Where the channels must curve, as on shell backs, particular care

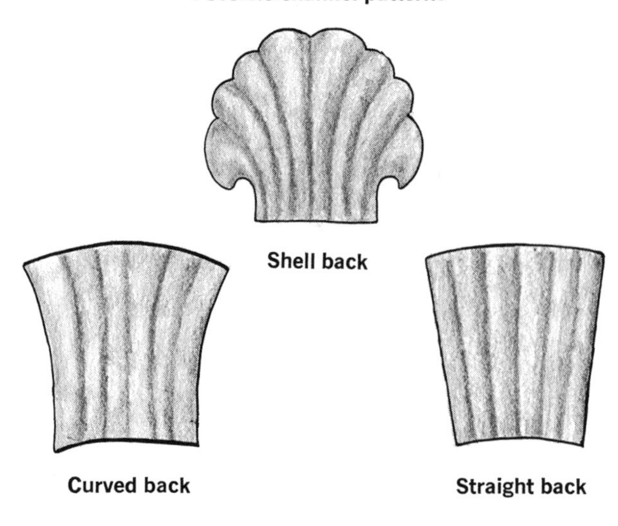

must be taken that all channels are equal in width. Any variations are noticeable. Mark the locations of the depressions between channels on the supporting surface.

Determine the desired channel profile. Center thickness should be 2 inches or more but may be varied for specific effects. For instance, backs that are too straight can be tilted back by thickening the bottom and flattening the top of the channels. Backs that slope too severely can be corrected by reversing the procedure. To measure the width of the channel cover, arch a steel measuring tape or cardboard tacking strip in the desired channel contour between the lines you have marked on the supporting surface. If the channel is tapered, measure at several points. Then measure the length of the channel from top to bottom. Allow extra length for channels that continue over the top of the back or arms and under back or arm liners to tacking points.

Make a paper pattern of each channel shape, using the exact measurements and allowing for 1-inch seam allowances and 3-inch handling allowance in the long dimension. A single pattern can serve for several identical channels.

These patterns will be used for cutting out muslin or final covers for channels, according to which of the three construction methods you use—muslin-encased channels under final covers, channels encased in final covers, or separate, prechanneled pads.

Muslin-encased channels

Muslin-encased channels are probably the best choice for the beginning upholsterer. The stuffing under inexpensive muslin channel covers can be regulated (see page 37), adjusted, or removed without the fear of damage that would accompany the same procedure for regulating stuffing directly under final covers.

Use the paper channel patterns for cutting out pieces of muslin. Place the muslin pieces in correct sequence, pin them together, and then machine-sew them together using 1-inch seams. Position the entire piece on the supporting surface; align a center seam over the corresponding mark on the supporting surface and slip-tack the bottom edge with a single tack through the seam line to the pull-through liner. Stretch the muslin to the top rail and slip-tack the seam line to its corresponding mark with a single tack.

Keep seam allowances together and point them toward the nearest side edge for back channels, toward the back for arm channels (see sketch). Lock-stitch (see page 23) the first seam line to the burlap-covered base. If you are channeling over a solid wooden base, use cardboard tacking strips over the

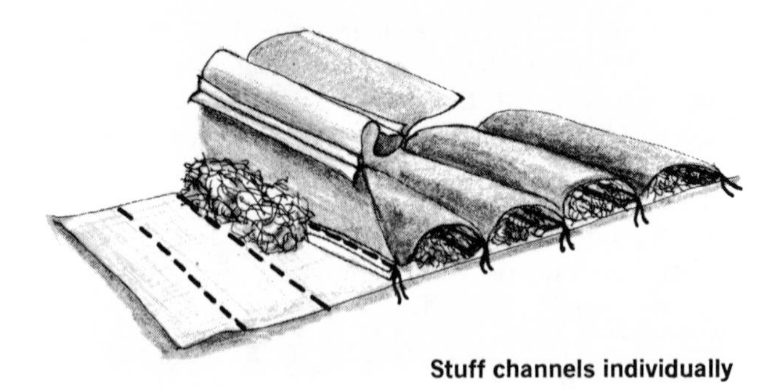
Stuff channels individually

seam allowances and blind-tack them to the surface. (See page 23 for details on blind-tacking.)

Raise the loose edge of the muslin channel cover and stuff with prepared hair, moss, polyester fibers, rubberized fibers, or foam. (Fibers are cleaned and prepared exactly as for normal stuffing—see page 29. See page 43 for special preparation of rubberized fibers and foam rubber for tufting and channeling.) Place enough stuffing under the muslin cover to produce a firm but resilient surface.

Starting at the bottom, use upholsterer's pins to fasten the seam line on the free edge to the corresponding line on the supporting surface; adjust fiber stuffing until you are satisfied with the effect, then lock-stitch the pinned seam line to the burlap. Leave tops and bottoms of channels open until all channels are in place.

Repeat the same procedure for the other channels. The outer channels may differ; if they are to overlap the outer edge, be particularly careful in checking shape and size, for any errors are especially noticeable here. In most cases the outer edges of the outer channels will be tacked down; slip-tack the edge and adjust stuffing before the final tacking.

Once all the vertical seam lines are stitched or tacked down, recheck for uniform stuffing consistency and shape. If necessary, regulate the stuffing. Add enough stuffing at the ends to form the desired contour. Where channel ends are covered by the seat, decrease the thickness of the channels to prevent gaps between channels at the seat line. Do not continue stuffing channels under back or arm liners. Tack bottom ends of channels to the back of the pull-through liner; where the tacked muslin could cause lumps in the final back cover, draw it around the back to the top of the liner for tacking.

Top ends of channels that go over the top rail should be stuffed for the best visual effect; often a fairly high crown is desirable to emphasize the fluted appearance. Slip-tack the center of each channel top to the top of the rail if there is to be a decorative panel along the top—to the back of the rail if the channels are to puff over the back edge. Determine how much channel muslin width will have to be taken up by pleats to produce the desired contour at the top edge. Rip out vertical seams far enough back to facilitate pleating. Plan all pleats to fall at channel seams; pleat slightly less than a quarter of the excess muslin width for a channel toward the center of the channel, and then use a single covering pleat back toward the edge to present a smooth outer surface. Overlap between the pleats on adjoining channels should face toward the nearest outside edge of backs and toward the

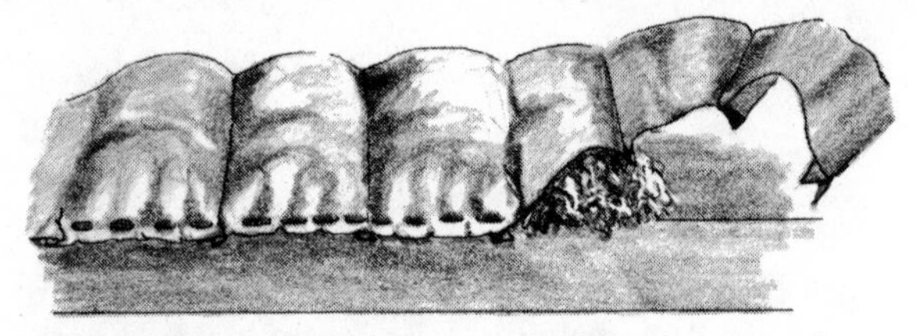

END PLEATS should face toward the nearest edge.

backs of arms. Use slip tacks for initial pleating; adjust pleats as necessary, drive tacks home, and trim off excess muslin. Channels that end at exposed wood are trimmed to allow a ½ to ¾-inch turn-under for tacking, usually to a recessed strip below the exposed wood. Slip-tack the turned-under edge, regulate stuffing, and drive the tacks home. Use the smallest tacks that will hold the muslin securely.

Final covers for muslin-encased channels are cut and joined exactly as muslin casings are. Be careful at all stages to align the grain of the fabric with each channel cover. If the bottoms of the channels disappear behind seats or cushions, you can cut costs by having the cover stop just below visibility behind the seat; use a 1-inch seam allowance and sew on an inexpensive piece of denim or muslin, commonly referred to as a stretcher, tacking extension, or pull-through.

For each seam, spread open the seam allowances and place a length of back-spring twine (cut a foot longer than the cover) on the seam, close the seam allowance, and machine-stitch a second seam. Use a zipper or cord foot on the machine, and run the seam as close to the string as possible without catching the string in the stitching. The seam should be just tight enough to hold the string in place; too tight a seam will result in puckers in the cover.

Drive slip tacks into the top of the seat rail between each channel. Lay a strip of felted cotton or polyester over each channel. The strips should reach

SEAMS USED IN UPHOLSTERY

Flat seams are used wherever the instructions simply say "sew together," or "sew a seam." A flat seam is made by placing the two edges of material to be seamed face to face, then stitching along a marked seam line or an even distance from the edge. A standard seam allowance is 1 inch; usually this is trimmed for neatness after sewing, but if the fabric is a type that ravels or pulls apart the seam allowance should be kept as wide as appearance allows. Unless otherwise instructed, spread the seam allowances open and press flat. Occasionally, for example for channel seams, both seam allowances are pressed in the same direction.

French seams (those used in upholstery have the seam allowance on the outside of the final cover) provide a bold seam and are occasionally used for period pieces and fancy covers. Place edges together, wrong sides facing out, and make a simple flat seam ¼ inch out from where the final seam line will be. Trim the seam allowances to about ⅛ inch; press seam open. Then fold the fabric back over the seam allowances on the stitching line, so that the wrong sides face each other. Stitch parallel to and ¼ inch from the first seam line, then spread material open and press seam allowance to one side.

Lap seams are used where raw edges on front and back sides are not objectionable, as for piecing burlap, denim, or muslin or adding hidden stretchers. Place the two pieces of material right side up, with edges facing. Slide one over the other about an inch and run one or more lines of stitches down the center of the overlap.

Folded lap seams are useful for joining fabric along a zig-zag seam line, as is necessary when you piece fabric for tufting. Mark the exact seam line on both pieces, then lay the pieces right side up with edges facing. Fold under the seam allowance on the right-hand piece at the seam line; it may be necessary to slit the seam allowance at corners or curves to keep the material flat. Slide the right-hand piece, with folded seam, over the flat left-hand piece. Baste or pin the folded edge on top of the seam line on the flat piece. Make one or more rows of machine stitching just back of the folded edge.

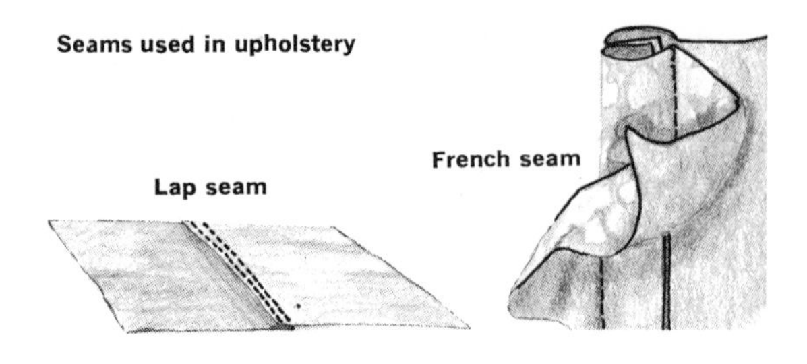

Seams used in upholstery

from seam to seam across channels, to the top and side tacking surfaces (but not onto them), and to the back and arm liners (but not around them).

Place the final cover over the padded muslin channels, and work each cover seam into the depression underneath it. Tie the bottom ends of the twine to the slip tacks on the seat rail. Use the twine to draw the cover seams smooth and tight and slip-tack the twine on the back or bottom of the top rail. Pull the bottom edge fairly tight and slip-tack it to the seat rail. Rip open twine-holding seams just far enough to prevent interference with twine or edge tautness at the bottom or twine and the top edge of the cover.

Smooth the cover and draw it fairly taut to the top (but not so taut that any stretcher material is exposed at the bottom). Keep the weave or grain of the fabric straight. Slip-tack the cover to the rail at the center of each channel, then work surfaces and seams taut and smooth, adjust as needed, and slip-tack in the final position.

Remove bottom edge slip tacks, slit the fabric to clear twines and their tacks, pull the cover tight, and slip-tack again. Loosen the twine along a center channel from its tack at the top rail, pull it taut over the back of the rail, and smooth the seam and adjoining channels toward the top. Retack the twine at least ¾ inch below the top or under the top rail. Repeat for each length of twine. When the entire cover is smooth and taut, drive the twine tacks all the way in.

Pleat and tack the top edge of the final cover in the same way the channel muslin covers were pleated, being careful to make neat pleats and keep grain of fabric straight. Minor corrections to fill out cover wrinkles may be made by adding padding *between* the cotton or polyester strips and the muslin. Use the flat end of a regulator, a small stuffing bar, or a tongue depressor to insert extra padding. Don't drive bottom-edge cover tacks in until you have checked the lower edge of the channeling against the completed seat or seat cushions to see if it is necessary to insert additional padding under the felted cotton or polyester to build up a more squared contact line between channels and seat. Then drive in the slip tacks that hold the bottom edge of the cover in place.

The final cover is tacked below show wood the same way as for muslin channel covers, except that gimp tacks may be used in place of regular tacks.

Channels directly under final covers

Prepare the final fabric cover like a cover over muslin-encased channels, but do not use twine at the seams. Lock-stitch cover seams to the burlap-covered supporting surface one by one as you proceed to stuff the channels, or blind-tack them to wood supporting surfaces. Stuffing the channels is handled differently than for muslin-encased channels. Line the underside of each cover channel segment with felted cotton or polyester torn to the exact length and width. Start at the bottom edge and insert moss or hair under the lined cover. Pin or slip-tack the loose seam of the channel segment to the supporting surface as you proceed to the top edge. Adjust the stuffing under the felted cotton lining with the flat end of a regulator or with a small stuffing iron. Then lock-stitch or tack the cover seam in place. Slip-tack the bottom edge to the seat rails. Complete filling the tops and side channels as for muslin and covers. Be careful to keep pleats neat and the grain of the fabric straight. Start each step at the center channel and work toward the edges; any visible overlaps should face the edges. For arms, start at the front channel and work toward the back.

Prechanneled pads

Prechanneled cushions attached to frames are often used in mass production as timesavers, but using them requires considerable initial planning in frame design to make the final effect look as neat or tight as channeled-in-place pieces.

Cut a piece of heavy spring-cover burlap the shape of the area to be channeled plus at least 3 inches handling allowance on each side and enough extra length to reach tacking points at top rail and seat rail. Position the burlap over the supporting surface, slip-tack it in place, and mark channel locations. Prepare the final cover as you would prepare a final cover over muslin-encased channels, then remove the marked burlap. Placing the cover over the marked burlap, start at the center channel and machine-sew the cover seams to the corresponding marks on the burlap. Turn seam allowances to the nearest outer edge on back covers, toward the back on arm covers.

Stuff the channels with rolled felted cotton or polyester, using a flat stuffing rod (see page 37). For a medium-soft channel, start with a strip of felted cotton three times as wide and 6 inches longer than the channel. A firm channel is built with a cotton strip five times as wide and 8 inches longer than the channel. Seat channels are usually made firmer than back or arm channels. Polyester, because of its greater compressability and resiliency, often requires half again the width you would use of cotton to achieve the same firmness.

Lay the stuffed pad over the supporting surface, stretch it to the desired shape, and slip-tack it to the frame. Adjust as needed, then drive the slip tacks home. Stuff the open-edge channels with rolled cotton or polyester and handle exactly as channels directly under final covers.

TUFTING

Tufting is the art of producing a pattern of mounds, usually diamond-shaped, on an upholstered surface. Buttons pulled tightly to the backing hold the stuffing down at various points to form the tufts. The upholsterer who likes to experiment with different visual effects can vary the basic tufting patterns—for instance, by using optical illusions to produce tufts which seem to be the same size but actually are not.

Two basic tufting methods are used—tufting a prestuffed surface and stuffing individual tuft pockets. The former is the easier for the beginning upholsterer to use in obtaining uniform shapes and stuffing consistency, especially if foam is used. If muslin stuffing covers are used, felted cotton or polyester is used between muslin and final cover. If there is no muslin cover between stuffing and final cover, a felted cotton cover liner is torn to match the tuft shape, and the stuffing is placed under the cotton.

Use of the diamond-shaped tufting pattern should be mastered before you experiment with more complicated shapes. Many variations in appearance can be achieved with this one shape by changing width, length, and height of the diamond and by combining diamonds in different ways. Channels can be used at the ends of diamond rows as an additional design element.

For simple, flat tufting surfaces, make a pattern of the surface shape on a piece of wrapping paper and use chalk to sketch in the proposed tufting design. Draw a center line from the top to the bottom edge and build your design symmetrically on either side of the line. Use the rough chalk layout as the basis for making an accurately measured layout.

COMBINATION of tufting and channeling was used on this chair. Note that pleats point down at tufts.

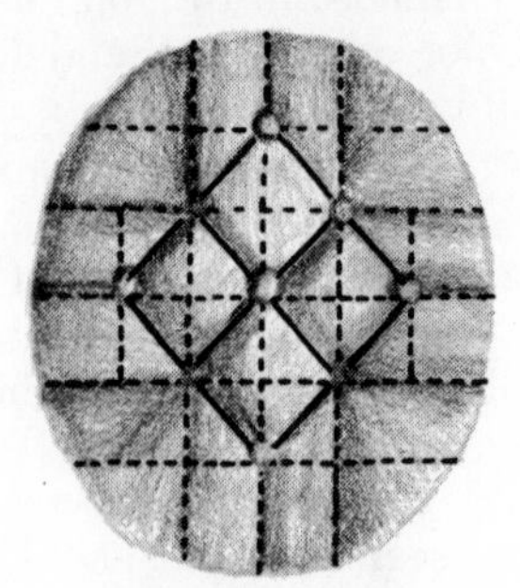

Four-square pattern

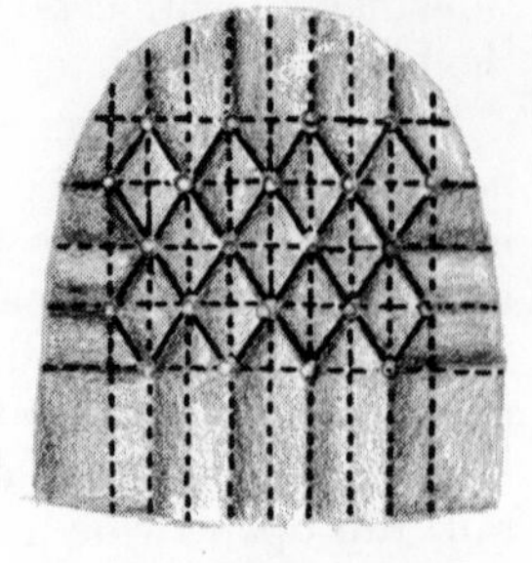

Diamond band pattern

Curved tufting surfaces are best planned by placing a sheet of heavy wrapping paper on the surface and tracing the outline. Cut out the pattern, tape or tack it on the rail edges, and chalk-sketch rough tufting patterns. Remove the paper and use it to make an accurately measured pattern.

Transfer tufting button points (the four corners of each diamond shape) from the paper pattern to the supporting surface by poking a soft pencil through the paper. Mark diagonal pleat lines from button point to button point. (A marking pen is excellent for this, except on final cover fabric.) Mark the button points on the back side of the supporting surface. A needle through the burlap or webbing locates them for marking; drill holes in solid bases to mark button points.

To determine what size the cover fabric should be cut, first measure the proposed shape of the largest tuft from button to button horizontally and vertically. Multiply the number of horizontal tufts at the widest place on the piece of furniture by the horizontal measurement of one tuft; add the distance from outer tuft buttons to tacking points, plus at least 6 inches handling allowance for each 1½ inches of stuffing thickness. This gives you the approximate horizontal dimension for cutting muslin or cover. The vertical measurement is obtained in the same way.

The best method of finding precise cover dimensions is to use an oversized piece of muslin; tuft it as you will tuft the cover, then trim off the excess carefully (preferably as a complete ring). The original cut size minus the trimmed excess gives you the correct cut size of cover materials. Leave enough final cover material for convenient handling.

Tufting a prestuffed surface

The surface to be tufted is prepared the same as any untufted surface, except that the top layer of stuffing must be highly resilient hair, moss, rubberized fiber, or foam thick enough to make tufts the desired depth, and the stuffing is built up around tufting twines.

For each button point cut a length of tufting twine 2 or 3 feet long, depending on the thickness of the stuffing. Make a single ¼-inch stitch across each tufting button point by poking the needle and twine down through the stuffing and burlap and drawing it back up to make two equal lengths on the stuffing side at each button location. Gently twist the pairs of twine ends just enough to hold them together. (If you must attach tufting twine to a solid base, drill ¼ to ⅜-inch holes through the base on button-point centers. Tack the center of a length of tufting twine to the underside of the base 1 inch from each hole, and use a long needle to draw the ends of each piece of twine through stuffing and casing ¼ inch apart. Proceed as for regular tufting.)

Build up a smooth fiber stuffing on the surface and around the twine, pulling twisted twines taut as you work. When the stuffing is complete, gently untwist the twines until they are separate. Use your finger or a stuffing regulator to make sure no fiber is between the twine pairs. Thread the twine pairs through the muslin cover ¼ inch apart (a crochet hook does the job faster than a needle) on their corresponding button point marks.

At all tufting button points which are the starting points for edge channels, knot a length of backspring twine to the backing and bring a single length up with the paired tufting twine for use as channel twine. The channel twine should be long enough to reach from the button location to the other end of the channel with several extra inches for easy handling. Pass it through the muslin casing on the channel edge line ¼ to ½ inch from the button point.

At the button point nearest the center of the area to be tufted, slip-knot the two tufting twine ends and draw up the knot until the muslin is in close contact with the stuffing surface but not pulled down into it. Repeat at each button point, working out from the initial point. Do not yet do anything with the channel twines.

Starting at the center and working out, tighten each button point gradually until the knot holds the muslin against the supporting surface. (It is best to tighten only a little at a time and repeat as needed instead of tightening a point severely, to prevent stuffing from shifting or snagging.) Difficulties in reaching the supporting surface may necessitate regulating the stuffing to provide a small opening in the fibers around the twine. Set slip knots and lock by adding an overhand knot. Trim free ends of knotted tufting twines. Pleat the folded material between button points by using the flat end of a regulator to shape the folds. Face pleat folds downward on backs and arms, to the free outer edge on seats and top surfaces.

Pull channel twines and muslin taut between edge channels, to check alignment; then fold twine and muslin back while you separate the stuffing fiber along the lines between channels by spreading and tearing or by cutting with scissors, then adjusting or trimming to prevent formation of a harsh edge. Place muslin back over the divided stuffing, pull taut along channel edge lines, and tack at the normal tacking point on the frame. Pull channel twine tight between channels, forcing the muslin down to the backing, then tack the free twine end at the same point as the muslin edge. Pleat and finish channels as described on page 41. There may in effect be horizontal channels between the last tuft and the sides of a frame; lap any horizontal channel pleats toward the bottom.

Foam or rubberized fiber simplifies installation of both stuffing and twines. Cut slab stock to the shape of the supporting surface, plus upholstery allowance (see page 34). Mark the locations of the tufting button points on both front and rear of the backing surface. Cement the foam slab to the supporting surface, or use tacking tape. Mark tufting button locations on the foam; tear or punch 1-inch holes through the foam or rubberized fiber slab at each button point. The holes should center on the marked points on the supporting surface. If you prefer, punch holes in the foam before cementing, center them over the marks on the backing, and cement the foam in place. Attach tufting and channel twine as for fiber stuffing, except that twisting the twines is unnecessary. Thread twines through the muslin, tie down the stuffing, and finish as for fiber stuffings.

You can produce more clearly defined tufting lines and channel lines by slicing approximately two-thirds of the way through the slab between button marks and along depressions between channels.

Covers directly over prestuffed surfaces. Proceed exactly as for prestuffed surfaces under muslin, but use buttons instead of twine ties (see page 44). Cotton or polyester pads torn to the shape of each tuft or channel are inserted between cover and stuffing as described for pocket stuffing under covers.

Final covers for muslin-cased tufting. Double check the original paper pattern for size. Compare the amount of muslin that had to be trimmed off with the pattern as a guide to the most economical size to cut the cover. Mark the tuft locations on the wrong side of the material, then cut the cover to size.

You have a choice of two methods for applying cotton padding between the final cover and the muslin casing. The first method starts by tearing a sheet of padding slightly larger than the tufted surface. Center the pad, locate the four central button points, and tear 1-inch-diameter holes in the pad at each of these button points. Lay the outer cover over the pad with corresponding button points aligned. Attach buttons at the four button points after gently but firmly smoothing the pad and the cover into the tufting points. Use your fingers, a regulator, or a fork to tear or at least thin the felted pad along the button-to-button pleat lines prior to attaching buttons to obtain maximum cover penetration. Continue the process from button to button, working out from the central tuft. Thin or tear the cotton felt at any channel depressions.

The second method is slightly more time-consuming but preferred by some upholsterers. Tear small pieces of cotton felt to exactly fit tufts and channels. Place them over their corresponding muslin-cased tufts or channels as you proceed with buttoning. Press the cotton felt pads and the final cover smoothly and firmly into the tufting points prior to attaching buttons.

UPHOLSTERY BUTTONS

Buttons are used in several ways for furniture upholstery. They may serve as small padded panels, as at the end of round scroll arms. On tufted pieces, buttons are pulled down tight to the base to hold the stuffing in the characteristic tuft depressions. In other cases, buttons are purely decorative.

Buttons for upholstery come in a wide range of sizes and shapes. Upholstery material suppliers or upholstery shops will usually assemble buttons for a fee if you supply fabric. Most department stores carry button-making kits which can be used with fabrics up to medium weights. Some kits that come with lightweight stamped assembly tools can be made to hold even heavy upholstery velvet if a length of ⅛ or ¼-inch pipe is used in place of the supplied tool to press in the button back. Mount the fabric cover on buttons so that grain and pattern will be in line with the fabric on which they will be placed.

Larger buttons can be made of shaped wood with cotton felt padding and cover fabric either folded under and tacked or sewed with a drawstring edge to be pulled tight on the bottom side. The upper edges of the button should be rounded off to a minimum of 3/16-inch radius. Wooden buttons can be drilled and threaded with twine before they are covered, or wire twine or cloth loops can be inserted for twine attachment.

Form a drawstring slip cover for a large button by cutting a piece of fabric 1½ inches larger in all dimensions than the button. Sew a line of small stitches with heavy thread or fine twine ½ inch from the edge all around the cover, leaving two long thread ends. Place the cover over the padded button base and tighten the drawstrings, keeping gathers evenly distributed to ensure a smooth top surface.

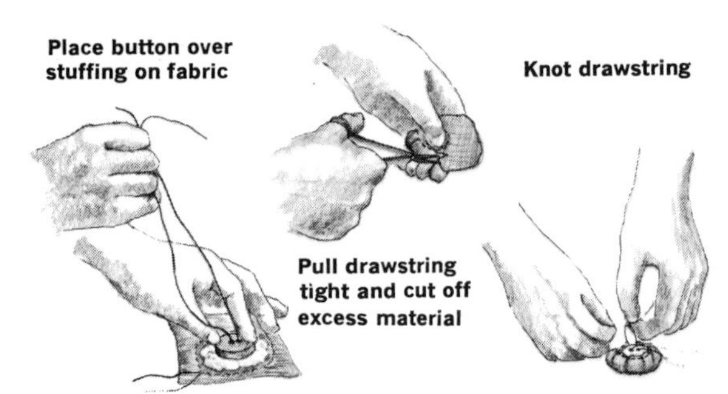

To attach buttons to a piece you are upholstering, thread a 2 or 3-foot length of twine through the button loop or tuft on each button so the ends are the same length. Thread both ends through a long needle and draw them through the cover of the piece to the supporting surface. Under a solid base (button holes must be pre-drilled in the base), pass twines around a slip tack an inch from the button hole, tighten and tie the twine, and drive the tack in. Under a fabric tufting base, place a walnut-sized piece of cotton felt between the two twine ends, pull the button down as tight as desired, and then tie the twine ends over the cotton with either a square or slip knot (see page 31).

It is possible to use tack buttons instead of twine-held buttons when you are tufting over a solid wood base. These are large tacks with fabric-covered heads. Drive small upholstery tacks through the muslin casing slightly off center of each button point to force the casing to the base but still leave room for the button tack. If there are edge channels, drive a slip tack ¼ inch from the button point on the channel depression line, tie one end of a channel twine to the tack, and drive the tack in; handle the channel twine as for normal tufting. Place padding and final cover over the muslin casing, smooth the cover into place, and drive a button tack through the cover and stuffing into the base at the center of each marked button point. If you use tack buttons on a piece without muslin casing, proceed as you would for regular buttons but drive button tacks instead of using button-holding twine. For channel twines, tack twine to the base, thread it up through the cover just off the button point center, and handle as for normal tuft channel formation.

Where channel depressions exceed 3 inches in length, especially if they go around a frame edge, stitch a channel twine into the bottom of each depression on the cover. First mark the portion of the pleat between channels that folds under along the bottom. Pull back the cover to the button at the end of the channel. Cut a length of twine 1 foot longer than the channel. Either tie one end around the button twine, just under the cover, or tie one end to the webbing and bring the free end up through the stuffing alongside the button twine. Fold the marked portion of the channel pleat in half, place the channel twine in the fold, and handstitch a line of ¼-inch stitches ⅛ to ¼ inch from the fold. From this point on, use the twine as you would for normal channels (see page 40). It takes a little more care in adjusting the fabric along the twine to produce a wrinkle-free cover. Pull the twine taut and slip-tack it inside the frame, or tie it to the button twine. Slit the cover fabric between channels to simplify finishing the ends, as for normal channels. Use the flat end of a regulator to form channel pleats facing down.

Pocket stuffing under muslin

Mark the layout of tufts on front and rear faces of the webbed or burlap-covered base and the muslin (see page 42). Align a center button mark of the bottom row on the muslin with the corresponding mark on the base. Use tufting twine to tie the button point to the base. From the muslin side, make a single ¼-inch-wide stitch through the muslin and webbing or spring burlap, and tie so the muslin at that point is tight against the base. Repeat for all button points along the bottom row; then proceed to the next row.

The two rows will form V-shaped pockets, and those on the bottom will have channel extensions toward the bottom edge. Fill the pockets with small wads of stuffing, placing them one at a time; stuff each pocket to equal density. Then tie down the third row of button points and continue stuffing. Keep repeating until the last row is completed.

V-SHAPED tuft pockets are individually stuffed; top halves are filled after next button point row is tied.

Stuffing the upper half of the diamond-shaped tufts after the third row is tied down may seem difficult at first. There are several methods of doing this, and you will soon discover which works best for you. Some upholsterers build up an inverted V-shape with stuffing above the pocketed lower half before tying down the button in the next row, then add any extra stuffing and shape as necessary under the tuft folds with the flat end of a regulator. Other people prefer to stuff the upper half after tying down the button point, inserting and shaping the stuffing under the tuft folds. Still another method is stuffing under the tuft folds with the top button point tied down only partially; the button point is tied tight only at the final stages of stuffing.

Individual tufts must be of even density or cover wrinkles and poorly defined pleat lines may result. Stuffing must be firm and resilient enough to hold its shape but not hard.

Work the flat end of a regulator along the diagonal lines between button points to produce pleats facing down. The open diamonds at the perimeter of the tufting pattern can be stuffed and finished like the ends of channels (see page 39) if the distance between the last button point and the frame tacking point is 3 inches or less. If this distance is longer than 3 inches, either stitch the muslin to the base along the channel edge line or use channel twines as described for prestuffed surfaces (page 43), then stuff to match the tuft pockets. To obtain the best appearance at channel ends, it may be necessary to slit the muslin along the channel edge lines. Check and correct pleats and regulate stuffing to ensure even density and correct shape.

Attach the final cover as described on page 44 for muslin-cased tufting.

Pocket stuffing under final covers

Stuffing individual tuft pockets directly under the final cover is a method widely used in commercial pieces, since it saves time. However, with most cover materials, errors can't be regulated through the covers. Tufts must be taken apart back to the error point, cutting drastically into the time saved.

Mark the locations of tufting button points on front and back surfaces of the web or burlap base and on the back of the outer cover material. Proceed as for pocket stuffing under muslin, but instead of tying the button points to the base with knotted twine, you tie the buttons themselves in place. Tear a piece of felted cotton or polyester slightly larger than each tuft or edge channel and place it against the underside of the cover before you attach buttons and insert stuffing. See page 44 for procedures for attaching buttons.

Final Covers

Because of the visual importance of the final cover, you should choose the fabric carefully and pay particular attention to the quality of workmanship that goes into cover application. Before you decide on a cover fabric, go on a tour of stores carrying the best quality furniture in your area. Examine various pieces, taking notes on the fabrics, seams and blind-tacked areas, fiber content, colors, patterns, and decorative features such as tufting, buttons, channeling, trapunto, or quilting (see page 51). Talk to the stores' interior decorators about fabric characteristics. Then visit several upholstery shops; if you don't take up a lot of time and have questions thought out in advance, professional upholsterers will often give you valuable tips and suggestions.

Using the notes you have taken, look through some fabric samples and decide on the combination of color, pattern, and texture that best fits your project and its eventual surroundings. You may be able to take the samples home overnight so that correctness of color shade and texture can be checked.

WHAT TO LOOK FOR IN FABRICS

Upholstery fabrics are grouped in three categories according to weight. Heavy fabrics include chenille, crewel embroidery, frieze, matelasse, needlepoint, plush, quilting, tapestry, tweed, velour, and velvet. Among the medium-weight fabrics are brocatelle, corduroy, damask, linen, monk's cloth, sail cloth, satin, and ticking. Fabrics usually classed as lightweight include broadcloth, chintz, denim, muslin, moire, sateen, and silk. Fabrics not specifically made for upholstery seldom have the durability of upholstery fabrics.

Heavy materials generally are easiest to install, and they hold tuft and channel pleats best. Their thickness can result in lumpy corner pleats if extra care is not taken. With the very heaviest fabrics there could be a problem when sewing through more than two thicknesses on a home-type sewing machine.

Medium-weight materials are almost as easy to handle as the heavy ones, and they are less likely to produce bulky corner pleats; however, tuft and channel pleats are not as well defined.

Lightweight materials are prone to ripping during installation and use, and they seldom produce visually satisfying tufting pleats. On the other hand, their lightness makes for easy handling on smooth surfaces.

Fiber content

Fiber content is a good clue to a fabric's durability. Cotton is still considered the best by many craftsmen for durability, though polyester fibers are beginning to be strong favorites. The synthetics go by so many trade names and change so rapidly that you should ask an upholsterer for up-to-date information about them. Even some of the synthetic standbys like rayon and polyester vary greatly in quality among different manufacturers. A specific rayon may wear well on the surface, while another may take contact wear poorly yet work well for backing. Check fiber content percentages, and then ask about the durability of the fabric before you order it.

Pattern and color

Before deciding whether a fabric is right for the piece you are upholstering, you need to know the size of the fabric pattern and how often it repeats. Samples may be too small to show a repeat of the pattern, but often the backing sheet will give pattern size and repeat information. A pattern that repeats every 24 inches is obviously too big for 10-inch cushions, and a pattern that repeats every 4 inches may be too busy for a large overstuffed chair.

For some pieces you must also know whether or not the fabric can be "railroaded." Railroading refers to cutting the covers so that when they are

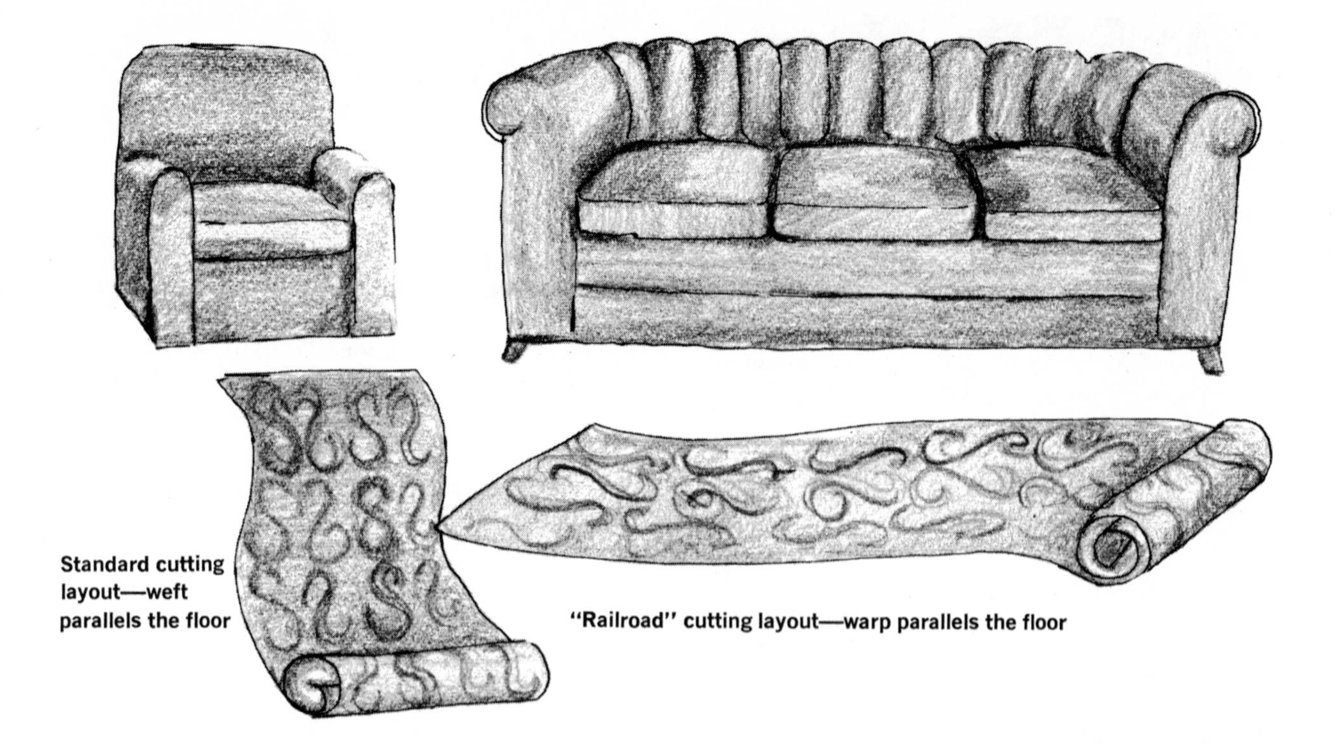
Standard cutting layout—weft parallels the floor

"Railroad" cutting layout—warp parallels the floor

installed the warp (lengthwise threads) of the material parallels the floor. Standard layout results in the width of the fabric paralleling the floor. Railroading often is necessary where long, unpieced panels are needed across a wide chair, a love seat, or a sofa. Most fabric patterns are designed to have definite pattern tops and bottoms in line with the warp of the material, so you will be restricted in your choice of patterns if you must railroad the fabric. Pile fabrics such as velvet, mohair, and velour are not good choices for railroading, since they have a definite up and down in the way the pile lies.

Keep in mind the period, scale, and shape of the piece you are upholstering when you choose a patterned fabric. Large patterns can overpower some pieces. Small, bright patterns can look busy, especially if there are many color contrasts in the pattern. Small or medium-sized patterns in subdued colors and contrasts can be used like plain-colored fabrics, but the texture of the pattern adds visual warmth.

Stripes accentuate the dimension in which they run; vertical stripes heighten and horizontal stripes broaden. Intersecting stripes can be visually confusing, so it is best to have all stripes on a piece running in the same direction.

Consider texture the way you do pattern. A dainty boudoir chair of Marie Antoinette's time would look as odd with a heavy tweed cover as would a heavy Cogswell chair with watered silk covers. This doesn't mean there may not be more than one texture suitable for a piece, however.

The choice of color depends largely on personal preference. However, there are some guides to consider. Bright colors over large areas tend to make furniture seem larger or more important than darker or softer hues. At the same time, they may seem overpowering for some pieces. Bright colors are most safely used on small or accent pieces. Neutral or soft colors will fit into more situations than bright colors.

Trim

Trim should be coordinated with the color, pattern, and texture of the cover material. Welt (see page 50) made of the cover material has a tailored look. Welt of a contrasting color or a stripe often gives an informal or modernistic look, while welt of the same color but contrasting texture can give a severely tailored look.

Brush or boucle edgings and bullion fringe (most yardage stores have samples) produce strong texture contrasts which can be either severely formal in appearance on appropriate period pieces or just fussy-looking.

Gimp tape is most often used as decoration in colors matching or complementing the cover. It should be chosen so that its texture or pattern does not clash with any texture or pattern on the cover.

Skirts and ruching are similar, though they differ in scale. Skirts hang toward the floor, adding visual weight, and ruching reaches out and up as a box-pleated fringe, adding a certain softness. Use both

DARK WELTING of vinyl artificial leather adds contrast to an otherwise plain, linen-covered couch.

with care so that they don't interfere with the lines of the piece.

PREPARING THE COVER

It is not wise to use the original cover as an exact pattern for cutting out a new cover, because it most likely has been stretched in use. However, the original cover pieces are good guides for shapes and for seams, tacking, and stretcher allowances. It is a good idea to code each piece for identification.

Measuring for covers

For purposes of measuring covers, length always refers to the dimension that parallels the top-to-bottom pattern or grain of the cover fabric as it will be used on the specific piece. Width is the dimension at right angles to the length. Normally the length direction is the same as the length or warp of the fabric and the width direction the same as the width of the fabric. When cutting fabric, measure width first, as this is the limiting dimension that determines whether you will have to piece fabric. When railroading fabric (see page 46), measure the length first.

Measure all distances from attaching point to attaching point, whether attachment is to be by tacks or stitching. Measure how long any stretcher extensions would be (see page 40), but don't deduct for them at this point; they will only be used if they actually allow you to save cover fabric.

Make a reasonably accurate sketch of each cover piece being measured and write in the measurements as you take them. Add standard 1-inch seam and 3-inch handling allowances. For reference it is handy to mark "S" along seam edges and "T" along tack edges and add an identification code for each piece. Measure all shapes as if they were rectangles.

Dotted line shows actual shape

Over muslin-encased stuffing, measure with a flexible tape measure held firmly across the muslin but not depressing it. Over loose stuffing, use the tape to hold down the stuffing until it is in the approximate profile intended for the cover at that point.

Pleated skirts and ruching strips are measured with the long dimensions as the width and the narrow dimension as the length. Refer to the sketch on page 49 for determining fabric width needed for each style of pleating. Allow 1-inch piecing seam allowances and 1-inch closing seam allowances. Length for normal attachment (¾ inch above bottom edge of the chair) will be the distance from bottom rail to the floor plus 3 inches for hem, top tacking, and handling allowances. If the skirt must be attached higher than ¾ inch above the bottom edge, add the additional length. For ruching strips, the length (the narrow dimension) is twice the exposed height of the ruching plus 2 inches for stitching and handling. The width is determined the same as for closed box pleats.

Seat cushion covers are cut so that the top of the fabric abuts the back of the seat. Measure maximum dimensions and add seam allowances. For puffy down or polyester-filled cushions, add ¾ inch to both dimensions for extra fullness.

Boxing width on cushions is the distance around the cushion's top plus standard seam allowances for each piecing seam and final closing seam. Length is

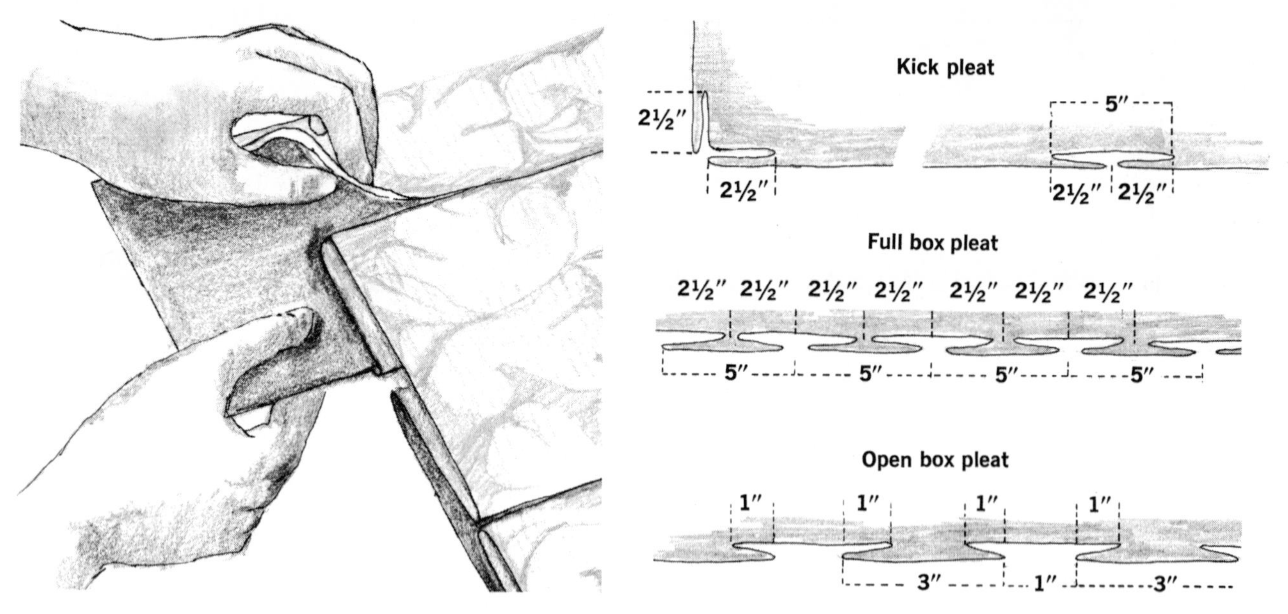

SKIRT PLEAT dimensions may be varied to fit work. The heavier the fabric, the deeper the pleat should be. Kick pleats should center on corners, cushion lines. Use cardboard spacer to fold pleats evenly.

determined by the desired edge thickness plus standard seam allowances for joining to top and bottom covers.

Fully boxed back pillows are measured the same as seat cushions. If boxed only at bottom and sides, the front, top, and back may be a single piece of fabric if the fabric has no definite nap or up-and-down pattern direction. If the fabric does have a nap and the cushion is to be reversible, a flat or welted seam must be used across the top to join separate front and back pieces.

Unboxed pillow thickness depends on the filling out of the joined top and bottom covers. Measure the space to be filled exactly as for boxed pillow top surfaces, and then add for filling out and handling allowance.

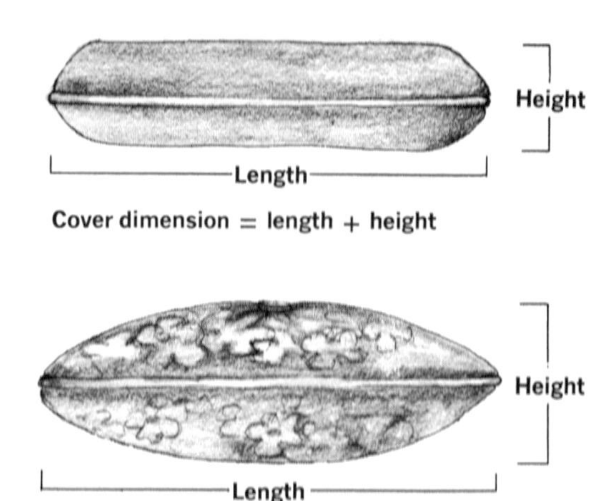

Cover layout and patterns

With measurements marked on your rough sketches, you are ready to make a cutting layout and pattern. The layout helps you achieve maximum economy in cutting cover fabric and prevents cutting mistakes. Make your layout on as large a scale as you can comfortably handle. Plain or small-patterned fabrics can be laid out on a fairly small scale, but for large or prominent patterns it is wise to make your layout as close to full scale as possible. Standard loose-leaf graph paper with four squares to the inch is ideal for most layouts. Tape several sheets together for long layouts. Let each square represent 2 inches on the fabric, or whatever scale suits the pattern of your fabric best.

Draw in the outline of the width of the fabric (54, 50, 48, or 36 inches depending on the specific fabric); leave the warp length open. If the fabric has large patterns, or even small or medium patterns with large background spaces, the major pieces (all large surfaces visible from directly in front and the outside back) must be positioned so the complete pattern is centered on each. Fabric patterns on boxing, borders, and panels used next to centered pieces should continue the pattern above or below them.

Mark the position of pattern repeat centers within your graph-paper fabric outline if centering is required, so that when you draw the cover pieces you can center them on the pattern. You will probably need an extra yard of fabric for every 24 inches across a seat front if a large pattern must be centered; a chair might need 1 yard extra and an 8-foot couch 4 yards extra.

HOW TO MAKE AND USE WELT

Welt is fabric-encased cord sometimes used to outline seam lines in furniture covers. Also called cording, welt is especially useful for hiding stitching irregularities where covers must be hand-stitched.

Single welt. Cover strips for single welt should be cut as long as possible. Though short lengths can be joined for welt covers, long strips look best. (If strips are pieced, press and trim the seam allowances at the ends. If material is heavy, thin cord by cutting some away where it crosses seam allowances, or seam the strips on a diagonal.) The width of the cover strip is determined by the cord diameter—2 inches plus three times the diameter of the cord.

Place the cord down the center of the strip and fold the strip over it. Then sew as close as possible to the cord, using cord or zipper foot on the sewing machine.

If welt is to be machine-stitched into a seam, place the welt between the two pieces of fabric, with the cord just inside the seam line and both welt and fabric seam allowances facing the same direction. Stitch as close as possible to the cord. If the seam is to be hand or blind-stitched, first sew the welt to whichever panel of fabric will be most directly visible on the finished piece, so that the blind stitching will be behind the welt.

Self welt. Encasing cord in a folded edge of one of two pieces of fabric to be seamed together produces self welt. Usually this method is less desirable than regular single welt unless your sewing machine has difficulty sewing through four layers of fabric, since it is hard to make a self welt look as good as a separate single welt. If you do use self welt, add three times the diameter of the cord to the 1-inch seam allowance on one of the two pieces of fabric to be seamed. Place cord just outside the marked seam line on the wrong side of the fabric with the wide seam allowance. Fold the edge back over the cord so it extends an inch past the seam line. Place both pieces of fabric right side with the cord edge of the one piece just over the marked seam line on the flat piece of fabric and the two seam allowances together and facing the same direction. Stitch as close to the cord as possible, using cord or zipper foot on the machine.

Double welt. Occasionally double welt is used like single or self welt and is sewn into seams, but more often it is used in a manner similar to gimp tape and is gimp-tacked or glued over cover tacking lines at exposed wood edges. It can be formed around commercial double welt filler, twin cords, or large, very soft single cord. Commercial double welt filler has a cross section much like a capital B. Cover strips are wrapped around the filler with some overlap on the back. One or more lines of machine stitches are then run down the center between the raised edges.

For twin-cord construction, cut cover strips to a width equal to 2 inches plus seven times the cord diameter. Place the first cord in the middle of the strip, fold the fabric over, and run one or more lines of stitches close together with the first as close to the cord as possible. If the welt is to be stitched into a seam, place the second cord up against the stitching between the cover-strip edges and stitch as close to the cord as possible. If the welt is to be tacked or glued at exposed wood edges, cut away all but 1/16-inch bottom lip, fold the top tightly around the bottom, and stitch between the cords as close as possible to the second cord. Trim off excess material.

Very soft, large-diameter cord can be made into a rather heavy double welt by wrapping it in a cover fabric strip, pressing flat, and stitching down the center one or more times.

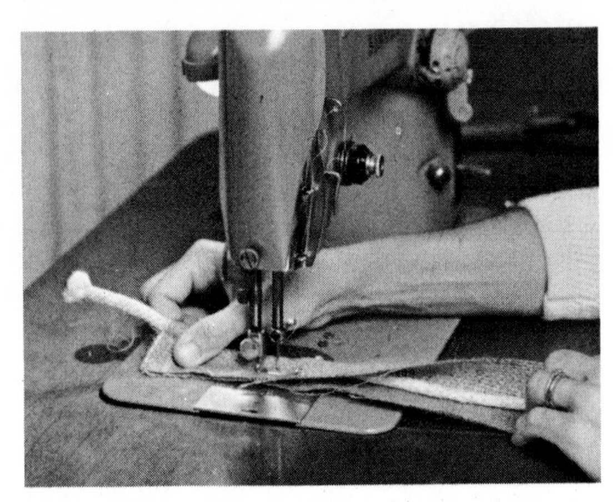

SEW WELT with a zipper or cord foot on the sewing machine; stitch tightly against the covered cord.

DOUBLE WELT can be formed by placing twin cords on ⅝-inch-wide masking tape, covering with fabric.

Start drawing the outlines of the cover pieces in the outlined fabric width on the graph paper. Be sure to draw the pieces with the top (grain direction) of each toward the top of the fabric. Start with the widest and visually most important pieces. Experiment until you have found the layout which requires the least amount of fabric.

If by shortening the cover fabric and adding stretcher extensions (see page 40) a savings can be made in the total yardage needed, use stretchers. However, if the shortened pieces would still have to be cut from the same amount of fabric, there is no reason for sewing on stretchers. Inexpensive denim, muslin, used cover material, or ticking is used to make stretchers.

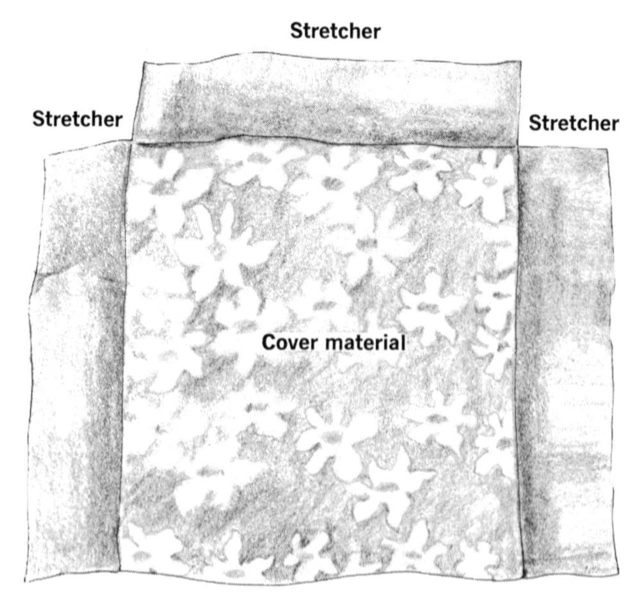

STRETCHERS may be used as tacking extensions on expensive cover fabric if hidden on finished piece.

Transfer the final layout to the fabric, using a yardstick and chalk to mark the outlines of the pieces on the right side of the fabric. Mark the top edge of each piece; also make a mark on the back identifying the piece.

Until you become more experienced, make a full-size paper template the exact shape of each piece that must be centered on the fabric pattern. Tear or cut a small hole at the visual center on the template, locate the pattern center on the fabric, and position the template on the fabric in correct relation to the grain or pattern, with the pattern centered in the template hole. If your layout of pattern centers was accurate, the templates will fall within the outlines you have chalked onto the fabric.

Cut the fabric along the chalked lines. Don't try to save time or material by cutting to the template. Often you will need the excess material for easy handling.

Sewing and decorating techniques

Most sewing on final covers (except cushions) is done by hand. Most often blind stitching is called for, though occasionally running, back, overhand, and tack stitches are used. Machine straight stitching is used for pull-over type covers, welting, edge finishing to prevent raveling, and decorative techniques such as quilting, trapunto, and false channeling. If you have a zig-zag machine, you can use a zig-zag stitch along cut edges to prevent raveling (though a line or two of straight stitches also works well) or to make quilting or trapunto patterns.

Quilting is done by stitching through the cover fabric, a stuffing, and a backing of thin muslin or cambric. The stuffing traditionally used is cotton, but polyester, rubber, and polyurethane foam are becoming increasingly popular. Stack the backing, stuffing, and cover fabric face up, then machine-stitch with matching or complementary thread around patterns in the fabric or in any designs you wish. Use a standard presser foot on the machine and make long stitches for a softly quilted effect. Short stitches produce a sharp stitch line which looks harsh on many fabrics.

To produce uniformly spaced parallel straight or curved lines, use a standard quilting attachment or attach a stiff wire quilting pointer to the machine. Draw a chalk line across the center of the area to be quilted, stitch along that line, adjust the quilting pointer for the desired spacing, and sew the next

Quilting layers and layout

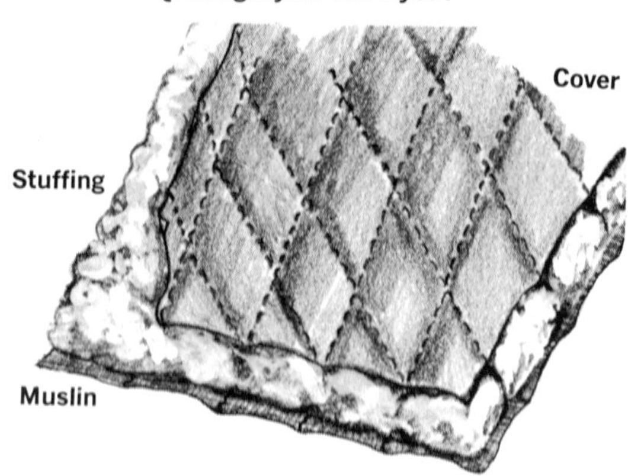

line while following the original line with the pointer. Repeat until one half is complete, then turn the fabric and do the second half.

Trapunto is a specialized form of quilting in which a single raised tube or band of quilting is produced between two parallel rows of stitches. It is used in upholstery to add the richness of raised design to plain covers and is popular as decorative detailing in quality women's fashions. Centering of the quilting design for trapunto is as exacting as centering

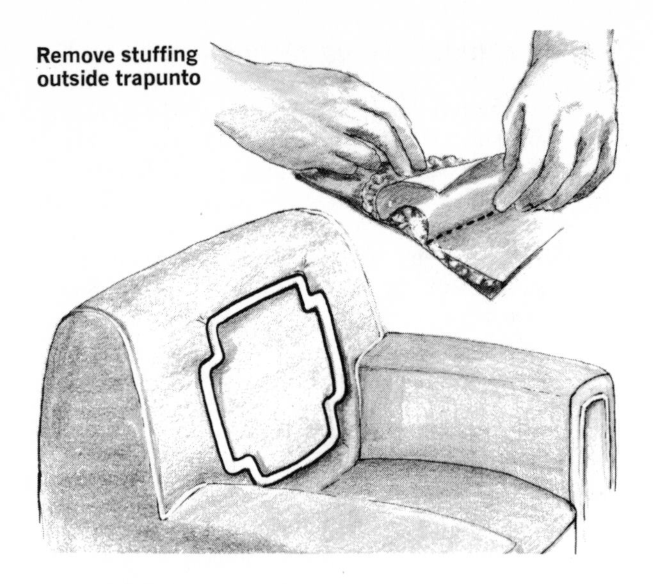

of large fabric patterns. Be accurate in your design layout and cover installation.

Just before installation, after all machine-sewn seams and welting have been completed, place the cover face down on a table and plan the trapunto design centered visually on the piece. Using chalk, draw horizontal and vertical center lines; the visual center of the piece is where the two lines intersect. Cut a strip of muslin or nylon net 2 inches wider than the space between the design's stitch lines. Place strips of stuffing (cotton, polyester, or foam) the same width as the muslin strip between the design's stitch lines. Use upholsterer's pins or tacks to fasten the cover, stuffing, and muslin in place, then machine-stitch with color-matched thread along all design stitching lines. When complete, remove stuffing materials not enclosed between lines of stitches and trim the muslin close to the stitching lines.

False channeling is produced by making long rows of stitching through the outer cover, stuffing, and a muslin backing. The stitching holds the stuffing down, so that the raised sections look like channels (see page 38). Polyester or soft or extra-soft foam 1½ to 2 inches thick is placed between the wrong side of the cover and the muslin backing, then machine-stitched with medium or long stitches to make the depressions between "channels." The foam or polyester is compressed to practically nothing under the stitches, producing a rounded line between the channels. If the foam is sliced from the top to within ⅛ to ¼ inch of the muslin side along the proposed stitch lines before stitching, sharper edges will be formed between channels.

INSTALLING THE COVER

Installing the final cover is much like installing a muslin cover (see page 35), with added emphasis on procedures for producing a smooth, neat surface. Stuffing must be free of lumps and voids; except with some rough-textured fabrics, any attempt to use a regulator through most cover materials will leave a permanent mark. Use the tacking method explained on page 36 to prevent pull marks, and make several small, flat pleats instead of fewer, more bulky pleats. Pleats on the front and top should face the nearest corner. Side pleats should face the back of the piece.

Be very careful to keep covers clean. An ink or oil smudge is difficult to remove, and a drop of glue will permanently stain a velvet cover.

Where covers must be fitted around corners and obstructions such as back posts, arm stumps, and legs, position the fabric and then slip-tack it from the center of each side to within a few inches of the obstruction. Smooth the fabric up to the obstruction and mark the contact points between fabric and frame corners. The drawings below show methods of cutting and folding fabric to fit. Cuts should stop just short of marked fabric-corner contacts so that the raw edge can be rolled under.

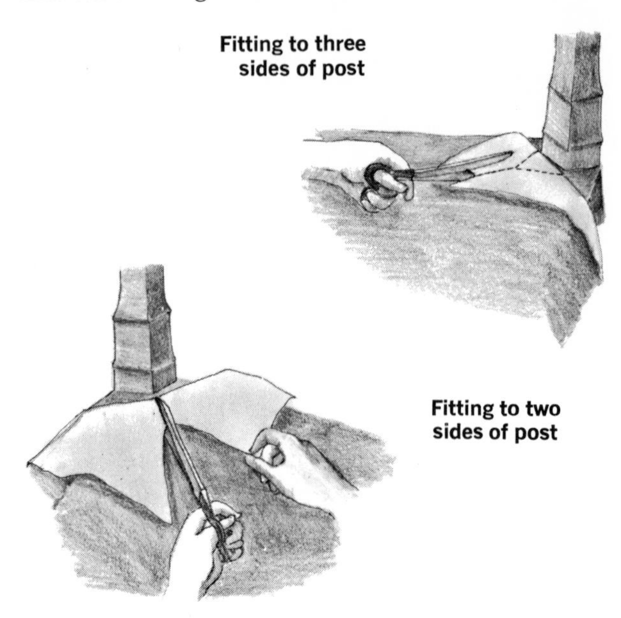

The order in which you can attach cover pieces can vary from project to project—a good reason for taking notes on disassembly order when reupholstering. However, most projects follow this order: seat, inside arms, inside wings, inside back, cushions and fitted pillows, outside arms, outside wings, and outside back. If arm and wing or back and wing are obviously a unit, combine them in the order. Backs often are built before arms and wings. Wherever there is a seam or a welt, make sure the seam allowances lie in the least visible direction.

In the instructions for final cover installation that follow, it is assumed that a muslin cover has first been installed over stuffing, unless otherwise stated.

Banding, borders, boxing, and panels

Banding, borders, boxing, and panels are used for anchoring stuffings, hiding rough edges, and providing linear accents to seats, backs, arms, or wings. Panels are used primarily to cover arm stumps and back or wing edges. Panels and borders may be installed as soon as all the adjoining cover pieces are installed, though they often are left until last.

Banding. Most often banding is used on spring-edge and platform seats. It is a separate strip of cover fabric used around the seat edge. The top edge is stitched to the exposed edge of the seat along the top of the spring-edge wire. The banding strip may have a welt or self welt sewn at the top edge. Align the welt with the top of the edge wire and turn seam allowances down; pin in place with upholsterer's skewer pins through the banding-welt seam to avoid marring the cover. Stitch banding to the muslin-covered seat with 1-inch running stitches through the seam allowances. Use felted cotton, polyester, or thin foam as stuffing under the banding from the stitching to within ½ inch of where the lower edge of the banding will be tacked on the face of the seat rail, or to the lower rail edge if it is to be tacked under the edge. Pull the banding fabric tautly and smoothly over the stuffing. If a border is to be used below the banding, tack the lower edge of the banding ½ inch below the top of the border location. If no border is planned, tack the banding under the rail. Use a regulator under (not through) the banding, to smooth the stuffing.

Borders. Borders are basically bandings, except that the top edge is blind-tacked to the frame instead of hand-stitched to the muslin or burlap-covered supporting surface. They are used where a strip of fabric can be wholly located on a framing member and tacked along both long edges. Borders often are used below banding on seat rail faces and to give a boxed effect on arms, the side of back posts, and the top of back rails. If welt is used it can be sewn along the top edge of the border or inserted when the border is tacked.

Blind-tack the top edge of the border strip to the top of the rail (see page 23). Insert felted cotton, polyester, or foam stuffing from the tacked edge to the bottom rail edge and then draw the border strip over the stuffing. Press stuffing toward the welt and regulate (under, not through, the cover) to prevent a possible void along the welt. Work from the center toward each corner, slip-tack the lower edge under the rail, and work out pull marks (page 36). Then drive the tacks in.

Occasionally borders are substituted for panels. Blind-tack the top border edge and attached welt to the frame, then tack cardboard strips over welt allowances (not attached to border) along the panel edge locations for the other sides. Stuff between welts and blind-stitch the three unattached border edges to the tacked welting.

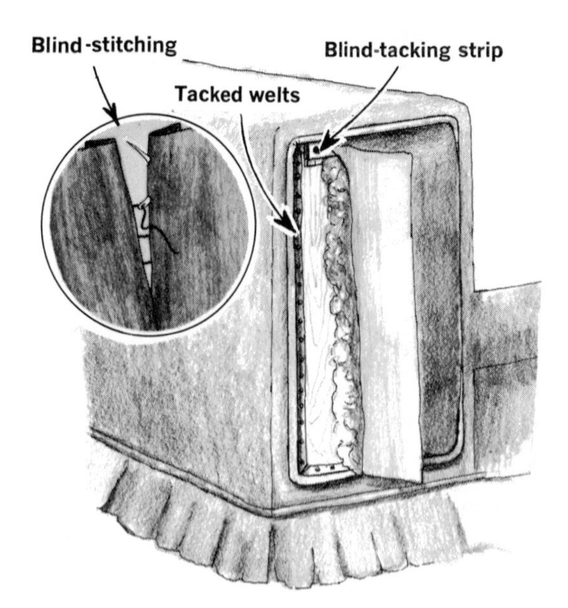

BORDERS may substitute for panels if stuffed and blind-stitched to welt as shown in this cut-out drawing.

Boxing. Similar to separate bandings and borders, boxing is machine-sewing two strips to the seat cover to make a single pull-over cover. Welt is sewn into the seam between the seat cover and the top strip (at the spring edge) and the seam between top and bottom strips (½ inch below rail top).

Align the top welt with the spring edge and lay the strips back on the seat so you can pin the welt to the spring edge and then lock-stitch the welt allowances to the burlap-covered base. Pull the seat cover taut and tack it at all hidden edges.

Place a felted cotton or polyester or foam stuffing strip between the two welts; bring the top cover strip down over it. Lift the lower strip of cover fabric back to expose the lower welt allowance, pull the upper strip taut over the stuffing, and slip-tack through the welt allowance with tacks 4 to 6 inches apart. Regulate the stuffing (under, not through, the cover) to produce a smooth surface; drive the tacks in, then secure the welt allowance further by blind-tacking it to the frame. Stuff and tack the loose edge under the frame edge exactly as for a border.

Panels. There are basically two ways of installing panels. Overlay panels are solid wood, plastic, or metal pieces that are padded and covered before being attached to the arm stump or back post. Stuffed-in-place panels do not use a separate panel support between frame and stuffing.

Plastic or metal bases for overlay panels are harder to handle than wood and are seldom made by the amateur. Solid wood panels, plain or carved, are fairly simple to make or obtain. The simplest are ½ to ¾-inch-thick slabs of wood cut to fit the required shape and then finished to match other exposed wood parts. Excellent carved panels can be made from carved or molded picture frames and decorative door moldings. Some moldings are even available in flexible form to fit curved surfaces.

Padded and covered overlay panels are made by cutting ¼ or ⅜-inch plywood to the desired shape. Cut a thin layer of cotton felt, polyester, or foam to match the shape of the plywood, and cut a piece of cover fabric 2 inches wider and longer than the plywood. Place shaped stuffing on the plywood, turn upside down on the cover fabric, and pull the fabric over the back of the plywood to tack it at the center of each edge. Working out from each center, stretch and tack the fabric to the back of the plywood along each edge. On outside curves you will have to make small pleats, and on inside curves you will have to slit the fabric at the edge to keep the cover smooth.

Attach the padded overlay panel to the supporting surface by using a regulator to spread cover threads at several points on the panel so you can drive finishing nails or brads through the plywood into the supporting surface. Use a fine-tipped nail to set nail heads below cover level; trying to drive in nails below cover level with hammer blows usually results in damaged covers. Use the point of a regulator to work threads back into place and hide holes.

Where using a regulator would permanently damage covers, cut the plywood for the overlay panels and then attach thin metal tack plates. Make the plates from thin but stiff galvanized sheet steel or aluminum, cut from tin cans or obtainable at most plumbing or sheet metal shops. Cut the metal to the shape of the plywood panel but slightly smaller to allow at least ½ inch of exposed wood all around. Drill holes or drive two-penny box nails through the plate at the points where you will attach the panel to the frame, position the plate over the surface to be panelled, and drive two-penny nails through the plate holes about ⅔ of their length into the frame. Withdraw the nails. Place a new set of two-penny

Nailing-plate assembly

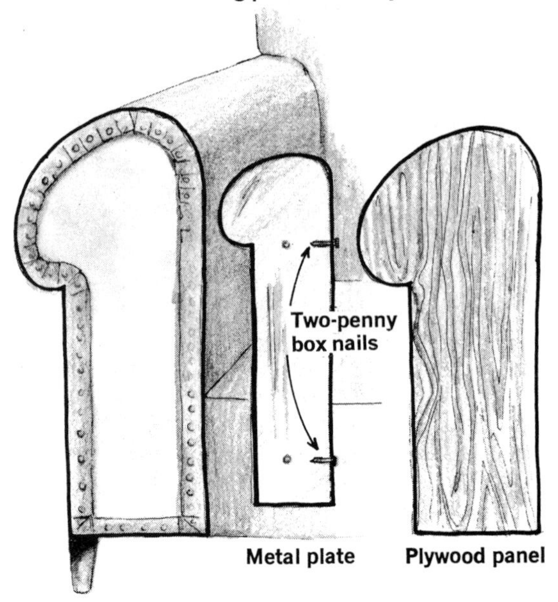

nails through the metal plate and cement the plate to the plywood panel form with epoxy or hot-melt glue. A few small tacks driven into the wood with heads overlapping the metal make good temporary glue clamps. When the glue has set, remove the tacks and stuff and cover the panel. Place the panel nails into the holes in the frame and drive them in, using a pad of soft wood or leather over the panel to protect it from mallet or hammer.

Another method that can be used to attach an overlay panel to a bare wood frame is to place sev-

AUTOMOBILE UPHOLSTERY

Automobile seats can be reupholstered or slip covered like any other piece of furiture. Because automobile seats are designed as separate back and seat sections, upholstering them is not difficult. Both back and seat almost always have pullover-type covers which are attached with hog rings to the springs, spring supports, or frames. If you have a heavy enough sewing machine you can use the false channeling technique described on page 52 to produce a bucket seat effect or any other quilt, tuft, or channel effect you want.

Use the construction methods described on page 61 for leather and leather substitutes when you sew automobile upholstery material. If you make welt yourself, plastic tubing should be used for the welt cores; it is available from most upholstery suppliers. However, readymade automotive welt, also available from upholstery suppliers, is much easier to use.

For seats that need new stuffing you can either duplicate the original stuffing or use more spring insulators and foam than the seat originally had. Extra stuffing can be added to raise the seat for a short driver, or the back can be reshaped for greater comfort. Many people find that an extra 1-inch layer of stuffing along the bottom 6 inches of the backrest makes the seat more comfortable, especially for long-distance driving.

eral beads of hot-melt glue on the back of the wood panel, then quickly position it against the frame. Hold the panel in place for a minute or two until the glue sets.

Panels stuffed in place can be made as described on page 53, using welt, or by the following method. Make a paper pattern of the panel; draw around the pattern with chalk on the furniture surface. Cut a piece of cover fabric with a 1-inch allowance all around the pattern. Fold under along one side and slip-tack to the furniture surface along the chalk line every 2 to 3 inches. Insert preshaped cotton, polyester, or foam stuffing under the cover. Fold under the remaining edges and slip-tack to the chalkline. Regulate stuffing (under, not through, the cover fabric) as needed, then drive in the slip tacks. Cover the tacked edge with gimp tape or gimp tape and ornamental tacks; ornamental tacks may be head to head or spaced (see page 23).

Seat covers

If a top stuffing of cotton, polyester, or foam is not already in place, one must be torn or cut to shape and positioned before the cover can be installed (see page 32).

Wherever a cover ends above exposed wood, insert stuffing under the cover just short of the tacking point. Turn under the fabric and slip-tack it at the centers of its sides. Then slip-tack out toward each end. Adjust the stuffing, smooth the cover, and drive the tacks all the way in. If the seat rail is to be completely concealed by the fabric, it is first covered with a thin layer of cotton, polyester, or foam stuffing reaching to (but not under) the bottom edge of the rail. The cover is placed over this stuffing layer and tacked under the bottom edge of the seat rail. Covers or their stretcher extensions are tacked to the tops of seat rails at seat edges hidden by closed arms and backs. When covers are worked around interfering arm stumps or back posts, tack the covers to within a few inches of the interfering member and then mark, cut, and fit as described on page 52.

Pull-over seat covers. Pull-over seat covers are generally used on round tied-spring seats, pad seats with edge rolls, and flat tied-spring seats with stitched edge rolls when all four sides are exposed or the back is fully covered. The cover fabric is a single piece which is centered over a muslin-covered supporting surface or top stuffing, worked smooth, and tacked. On pieces with fully covered backs, extend top stuffing 1 to 2 inches down beyond the contact line between the back and seat, then tack the cover to the frame at the same point as the muslin is tacked, where it will not interfere with installation of the back cover.

Welted pull-over covers are used in the same types of seats as plain pull-over covers and always with all four sides exposed. Welt is sewn to the face of the cover at the exact point where it lies against interfering back posts or arm stumps to give a more formal, finished look to a pull-over cover. Cut a paper pattern to fit the seat, making cutouts for posts and stumps so the pattern comes right up against them. Mark the exact center of front and back rails on the pattern. Place the pattern on the right side of the cover fabric. Mark the rail center points and the post and stump cutout on the fabric with chalk. The chalk marks at the post and stump locations are where the welt will fall. Slit the cutout waste to ⅛ inch from the corners. Where cover and welt will contact two sides of a post, sew welt to the right side of the cover along the chalk line at the corner and halfway down each adjoining side.

Welt location on pull-over covers

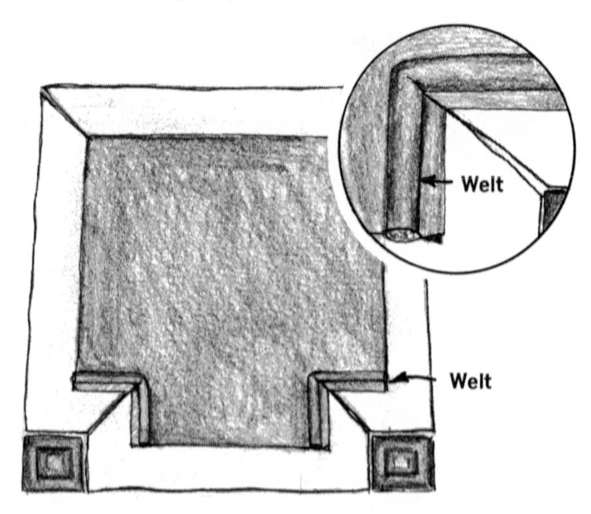

For covers that contact stumps on three sides, sew welt to the cover along the chalk line on the center side of the cutout only. Position the cover, align the center marks with the centers of the front and back seat rails, and fit the welted cutouts snugly against the posts and stumps. Use the flat end of a regulator to poke welt allowances down between cover and posts. Complete smoothing and tacking the cover as for a plain pull-over cover, but leave the last few tacks next to the posts until the welt is tacked down. Pull the welt tight against the post and draw the welt allowance down under the seat rail. Tack on sides of seat rail and under the seat rail. Where welt is not presewn to the cover, it may be necessary to blind-stitch the cover to the tacked welt for the best appearance, especially over seat rails.

Panels and borders (page 53) are often used with plain or welted pull-over covers. Mark the upper limit of the panel or border on the seat rail, tack the pull-over cover ¾ inch below this mark, and construct the panel or border.

Boxed covers. Both edge-rolled and spring-edge seats and backs may have boxed covers. Sometimes boxed covers with a single welt line are called banded covers, but they are actually a variation on the double welt line more often used with boxed covers. Banded covers are traditionally hand-stitched and used with spring-edge seats and platform seats.

Make a paper pattern for the cover by placing heavy paper on the seat and carefully marking the seat shape (at the outer edge on edge-roll seats or at the edge wire line on spring-edge and platform seats). The marked line is where the top welt will be sewn; on edge-roll seats the welt should follow the outermost edge of the roll, while on spring-edge and platform seats the welt lies along the edge wire and may be stitched through the welt allowance to the burlap at that point. If a second line of welt is desired at a lower point on the seat rail it can either be machine-stitched or added as a welted border below a single-welt boxed cover.

When fully closed arms and backs cover back and side seat edges, boxing continues only as far back as the arm stubs plus enough extra at each end to tuck between seat and arms for a neat finish.

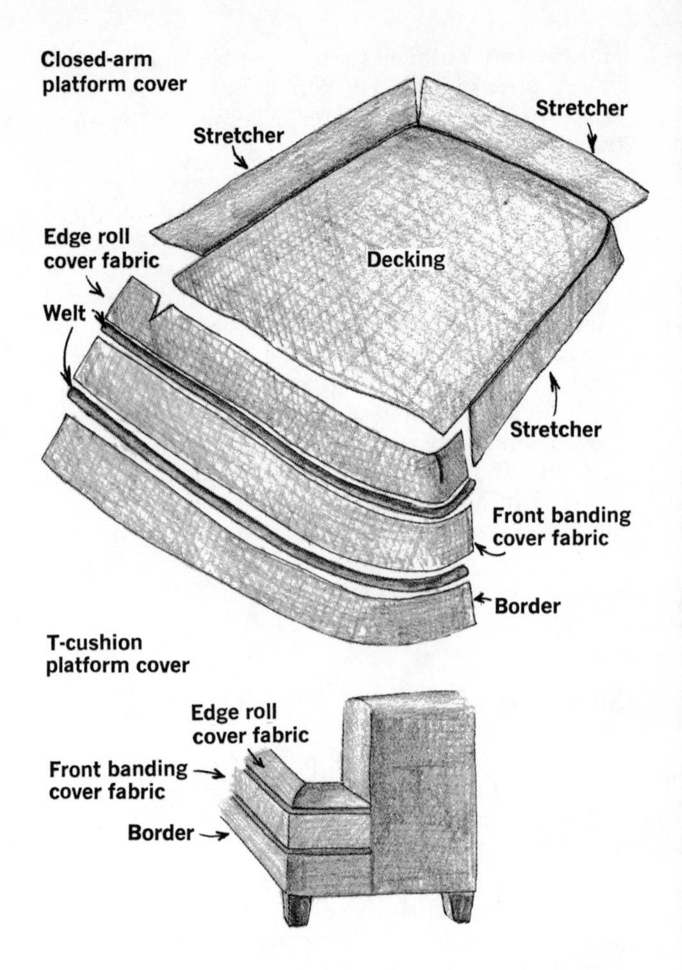

Banded covers. Banded covers are almost exclusively used on platform and spring-edge seats. For platform seat covers, first cut decking (denim or other sturdy but inexpensive fabric—usually in a matching or neutral color—used where a seat cushion will cover it) to reach from the rear edge of the spring-edge roll to the back seat rail and from side rail to side rail, plus seam and tacking allowances. Then cut a cover strip wide enough to reach from the rear edge of the spring-edge roll to the spring-edge wire, plus seam allowances. At return arms with T-cushion platforms, miter and machine-sew the corners. If top stuffing is not already in place, tear or cut a piece of cotton felt to fit from the back edge of the spring-edge roll to the back seat edge and from side to side. Tear another piece to fit from the rear edge of the spring roll to the spring-edge wire over the top of the roll. Tear strips to fit banding and border, if they are used.

Machine-sew the cover strip to the front edge of the decking, right sides together. With cover strip lying back over the decking, place the decking on the seat with the machine stitching aligned with the back edge of the spring-edge roll (seam allowances should be together, facing forward); pin to the burlap spring cover along the seam. Stretch and smooth the decking over the stuffing and slip-tack it to the seat rails. If necessary to get around hidden posts, split edges of decking or stretcher extension. Adjust decking as needed so that it is taut and smooth; then lock-stitch the pinned seam to the seat burlap.

Draw the cover strip forward over the edge roll and top stuffing and pin the free edge to the burlap along the spring-edge wire. Adjust the cover strip for a smooth, taut fit and then stitch in place. Follow the directions on page 53 for banding and border.

Banded spring-edge seats are built very similarly to platform seats except that cover fabric is used on the entire top instead of just in front of decking. Make a paper pattern of the seat to reach from the spring-edge wire on all exposed edges to all tacking points on the chair rails under closed arms and backs. Mark a line 2 inches under the arm and back overlaps for possible stretcher limits. Make an outline of the pattern on the right side of the fabric. Add seam and handling allowance and cut the fabric. If you intend to use stretchers, transfer the stretcher lines from the pattern to the cover, leaving a 1-inch seam allowance. Sew stretchers to fabric with double-stitched lap seams (see page 40).

Place a layer of felted cotton over the seat from spring-edge wire to seat edges. Lay the cover on the seat and align the front pattern line with the spring-edge wire; pin in place. Draw the cover taut and smooth and slip-tack the free edges to the seat rails. If hidden posts interfere, slit edges of cover or stretchers just far enough to clear the posts. Adjust the stuffing and cover as needed and then stitch along the burlap over the spring-edge wire. Install banding and border as described on page 53.

Inside arm covers

Arms may be either open with upholstered arm rests or fully covered with no open areas between the arms and the seat or back. Open arms usually have either a small pad on top or a fully covered arm rest. Occasionally you will find arms padded on the sides but open at the arm-seat junction. These may be handled like open backs if definitely separate from the back or like covered backs if obviously related to the back.

Open arms. Small padded arm rests are most often found on side chairs with French or "picture frame" backs. Tear a piece of felted cotton to fit over the stuffed and muslin-covered pad. The cotton should stop ¼ to ½ inch short of the bottom edge of the arm board or the exposed wood tacking point or rabbet to prevent lumpy edges and pull marks. Center the cover fabric over the pad, smooth it and draw it tight, and slip-tack it to the armboard at the back, front, and side centers. Slip-tack toward the corners on all sides. If pleats are necessary, make many small pleats instead of a few big ones. Smooth and tighten the cover and complete tacking. Tack close enough to the exposing wood edge so tacks can be covered by gimp tape or double welt trim.

If arm rests to be covered all around have been prepared with stuffing and muslin cover, a single layer of cotton felt should be torn to fit over the board down to and even with the bottom of the board. If the back of the arm ends under a T back, end the cotton felt just beyond where the arm meets the back. On bare boards, build up a slightly crowned surface of cotton felt, then apply a final layer to fit down to the bottom of the board on each side. Pull under the cover at the center of each side of the arm and slip-tack ¾ inch from the edge. Pull the center of the front edge under and tack it ¾ inch back from the edge on the bottom. Smooth and pull the cover toward the back; fit it to posts and back as described on page 52. The tabs may be turned up instead of under where other cover pieces will lap or meet the edge. The turned-up tabs provide insurance against the frame or the stuffing showing through. Pull the cover around the back post and level with the middle of the arm board.

Slip-tack the two sides, working from the center alternately toward the back and front; smooth, align, and tighten the cover as you proceed. Pleat the cover fabric smoothly over the front and tack ¾ inch from the edge on the bottom surface. (If the front of the arm has an exposed wood "knuckle," handle the front edge as you would the front edge on small pads.) Fit and tack the back of the arm. If necessary, add extra cotton under the existing top layer of cotton to fill out any gap between arm and back.

Make sure the arms match and then drive slip tacks in and trim off excess fabric. A cambric dust cover or even a piece of cover fabric used as a dust cover is usually added to the underside of the arm after all covers are in place (see page 60).

If you want the arms to have a more slender appearance, you can limit cotton stuffing to the top surface of the arm board. However, without cotton stuffing on the sides the arms are less comfortable to lean against.

Fully covered arms. Covers for arms that are fully upholstered are attached like muslin arm covers, except that back and bottom stretcher extensions may be used and the cover may be installed in several sections to permit banding, boxing, or borders. Cut cotton felt to cover the arm and tack it in place. Cotton felt is never placed over an edge unless it is extended well past it; to just barely extend the cotton felt over an edge would cause ripples and pull marks. Cotton felt should stop ½ inch from tacking points to prevent lumpy cover tacking. Extend the cotton just beyond where the back covers the arm and down just below where the seat or platform meets the arms.

If you want the grain of the cover fabric to parallel the floor, take into account the slope of arm tops when you cut out the cover. Position the cutout cover and slip-tack it at the center of top and bottom edges. The bottom edge of cover or stretcher is tacked to the top of the seat rail over the tacked seat cover instead of to the arm liner, where the muslins are tacked. Work forward and back from the centerline slip tacks, smoothing, tightening, and slip-tacking as you proceed.

Fit the cover around the back post if necessary. Pull the back edge over the arm slat and tack it to the front edge of the back post. With exposed wood arm stumps, finish for gimp or double welt trim as for seat covers.

On arm stump faces to be covered with panels or bordered false panels, pleat and tack the cover to the face of the stump far enough in so the tacks will be under the panel. Install panel or bordered false panel as described on page 53. If the panel is to be recessed, cotton should round stump face edges, preferably over an edge roll, and stop just short of the panel. If a large covered button or small panel is to be used only at the top, the arm cover is brought around the face of the arm stump and tacked on the back side of the outer edge of the stump to fully cover the front. Pleating or shirring a large button with twine is described on page 44.

Build boxing, banding, or borders to suit the shape of the arms (see page 53). A variation is constructing the boxed cover like a boxed loose cushion with one or more edges open instead of the bottom. This makes a pull-over cover for slim modern arms and backs.

Inside wing covers

Wing covers are often an extension of either the back or the arm covers, in which case they are attached with back or arm covers. For wings covered separately, position the cover over the stuffed wing (cotton felt should not overhang the outer frame edge of the wing unless an edge roll is used). Slip-tack or pin the covers at the center of each edge. Turn the bottom edge under where it joins the arm, slitting where necessary to match it to the arm shape. Pin the turned-under edge and remove slip tacks and pins above the arm, bring the top of the cover down over the seat, and blind-stitch the turned-up bottom of the wing cover to the arm cover. Slit and pleat the cover to fit smoothly, draw it taut, and slip-tack along top and front edges. Draw the cover over the wing slat and tack it to the front of the back or wing post; if there is no slat, tack the cover to the inside of the post.

Boxing and border shapes on wings tend to be a little more complicated than for seats and arms. Mark shapes and welt lines on paper patterns, or locate them on the cover fabric itself by pinning the cover in place, marking the welt positions, removing the cover piece, and attaching the welt.

IDENTIFYING COVER PIECES

When you cut out a cover, mark each piece with its name and function. An identification code such as the one that follows is useful. Mark on the wrong side of the fabric, using chalk or other marker that won't show through. On delicate fabric, some upholsterers prefer to staple or tie (with thread) a tag to a seam or tack edge or use the type of cellulose tape that you can write on. It will be helpful for beginners to add the identifying code of the adjoining piece along each edge.

The letters of the following code can be used in various combinations to describe the location and function of each cover piece. The first letter will always be that of the complete part—A, B, C, S, or W. To identify an outside piece, add O after the first letter. Use the function codes Ba, Br, Bx, P, R, Sk, and Wt after a dash. For example, rushing for a seam on the outside of the arm would be AO-R. Welt for the inside back and the outside arm would be B—Wt and AO—Wt.

A	Arm (inside)	P	Panel or facing
B	Back (inside)	R	Ruching
Ba	Banding	S	Seat
Br	Border	Sk	Skirt
Bx	Box	St	Stretcher
C	Cushion or pillow	W	Wing (inside)
O	Outside	Wt	Welt

Inside back covers

Apply felted cotton top padding to the inside surface of the back. Do not lap the cotton over raw frame edges, and stop it ½ inch short of the tacking edge on exposed wood edges or rabbets.

Open back covers. Covers for open backs are finished on all edges. For fully covered open backs, pull the edges of the inside cover around the posts, rail, and liner and tack to the inner edges of frame members, unless frame members are wide enough that the cover edges can be tacked ¾ to 1 inch in from the frame edge on the back. If banding or borders are to be used at edges, tack cover edges just beyond where banding or border will begin. Do not turn edges under when tacking to the back surface. If it is necessary to open seams to eliminate wrinkles, use a blind stitch to sew shut again. French or picture-frame back covers should be cut oversized, positioned and tacked, and then trimmed; if the tacking point is rabbetted deep enough, trim the fabric, turn it under, and then tack. If the back is curved (side to side), stretch and tack the cover to top and bottom edges before stretching and tacking it to the sides. If the back is scooped (top to bottom), stretch and tack cover to each side before tacking to top and bottom.

On normal backs, position the fitted cover, smooth and tighten it, and slip-tack it at the center of each side. Smooth and slip-tack out from the center tacks to all corners. Pleat the corners; slit and work fabric around the back posts as described on page 52. If the back contacts the arm board, fold the cover under and draw it tight before tacking at rear or inside of post. If properly tightened it need not be tacked to the arm, but it may be blind-stitched to the arm cover. When all wrinkles are eliminated, drive tacks all the way in.

Closed back covers. If the back continues down to the seat and its outside cover hides the back edge of the seat, it is called a closed back. (If cover edges are exposed, they are installed the same as for open backs.) If the edges are covered by seat and closed arms, they are tacked to the top of the seat rail and the inner edge of the back posts. Treat the cover ends for scroll or round backs the same as the ends of scroll arms, using a drawstring to shirr or pleat the ends and then covering them with panels, false panels, or buttons.

Continuous backs and arms may be found on relatively slim chairs and barrel-type chairs where a smooth transition between arm and back is desired. Close examination of most pieces will show that the cover is actually in three pieces; if a cover is made in one piece, the grain and pattern on the arms will not be parallel to the floor unless the back is uncomfortably vertical. Cut pieces so there will be at least 2 inches overlap between them when they are in position. Pin the back piece in place. Mark the desired seam location on each side of the inside back cover, along the front of the back posts on the arm to the bottom of the back. Pin arm pieces in place, matching pattern and grain. Then smooth the cover to the back and mark for seams along the same line used for backs. Remove arm and back pieces and trim to leave standard seam allowances beyond the chalk marks. Join the arm and back pieces with either French seams or welted seams.

Slip-tack the back cover at the center of the top and bottom edges to the back of the top rail and the top of the seat rail. Working toward both arms, smooth, tighten, and slip-tack the cover. Pull the fabric around the posts above each arm and tack on the inner side. Tack the back-to-arm seam in place, in line with the joint between back and arm frame. Then continue smoothing, tightening, and slip-tacking the cover out to the ends of both arms, handling tops and ends as necessary for the particular style of the piece.

Trim used at outside edges (such as welting, brush, boucle, edging, and ruching) is applied between the outside covers and the inside covers at the outer frame edge. Trim could be sewn to the edges of either the inside or outside covers before they are installed, but it is usually faster to use widely spaced tacks to fasten the trim to the edge over the edge of the inside cover and then tack or stitch the outside cover in place. Especially on irregular edges, it is easier to tack a welt to the edge (using a cardboard strip as for blind-tacking) and then blindstitch the back cover in place than to blind-tack the cover itself to an intricate edge.

Outside covers

Before proceeding to the covers for the outside surfaces, sit on the piece to test it for comfort and possible slackness or wrinkles. Correct any slackness or wrinkles in the covers for the inner surfaces before covering the outsides. Outside brush, welt, bullion fringe, buttons, panels, skirts, and ruching are almost always put on at the same time as the outside covers.

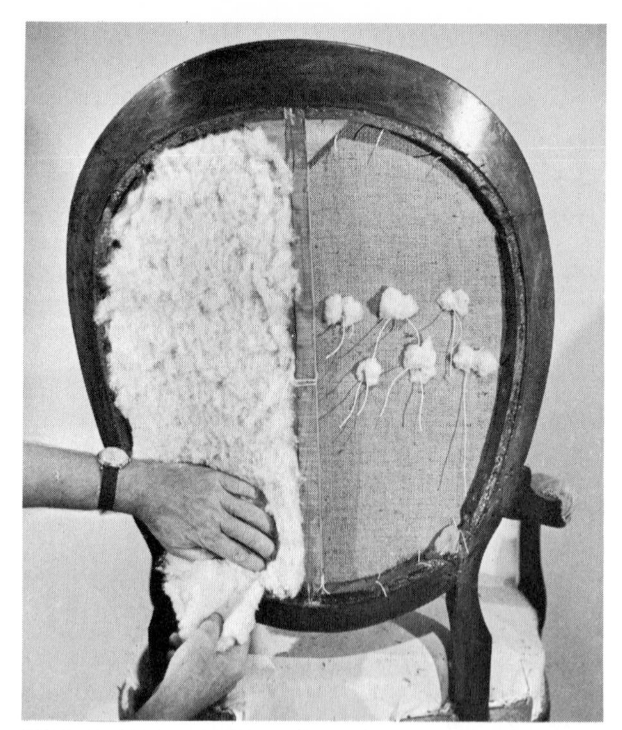

FILL SMALL VOIDS with stuffing to give desired surface shape and decrease the strain on the cover fabric.

If the outer face of the frame is webbed or solid, proceed by placing a thin layer of felted cotton over the surface. Tear the cotton to fit just back of the outside cover edge.

Open frame spaces must be spanned or filled to prevent the cover from being damaged under pressure. Small voids can be filled with loose stuffing and cotton. Larger spans should be webbed or covered with heavy, tautly tacked burlap, chipboard (an upholsterer's heavy cardboard), or ⅛-inch-thick plywood (most economically available as door-skins for resurfacing unpanelled doors). If burlap is used over very wide spaces like sofa backs, it is wise to add vertical and shaped wooden slats for intermediate support or to use vertical webbing every 2 feet behind the burlap. The burlap is tacked far enough from the frame edge that it won't interfere with cover tacking. Chipboard and plywood are best used in a rabbet, but they can be fitted 1 inch from the edge and padded enough so the edge line is hidden, or they can be added before the final tacking of the inside cover or borders and brought out to the frame edge, in effect deepening the frame.

If there is not room on the frame for tacking burlap and cover separately along the top, align the cover as if to blind-tack but insert the edge of the burlap under the tack strip before driving the tacks in. For the sides and bottom, attach cardboard and welt with burlap between them.

Place a layer of felted cotton over all frame space

fillers and the frame itself just short of the finished edges.

Wherever possible, outside covers are blind-tacked or blind-sewn on the top edge. Position the cover so fabric grain or pattern is straight and then turn under 1 inch along the top. If the top is not a straight line, you may have to slit it or cut out wedges from the turn-under to shape the top edge. Pin the folded edge firmly to the chair; then fold back the fabric and blind-tack it to the frame edge, using a cardboard strip. On irregular edges you may have to cut your own cardboard strip from chipboard or fiber board. (Pretacked metal strips are available for curves—see page 61—but are usually successful only for heavy fabrics and plastic leather substitutes.) An alternate to blind-tacking is blind-stitching the folded edge to the top rail trim, or gimp-tacking it to the rail.

Smooth cotton over the tacking strip, bring the cover back over the outside of the chair, and pull it smooth and tight at the center of the bottom edge. Slip-tack it on the underside of the seat rail at the center and then work toward the legs, smoothing, tightening, and slip-tacking the cover under the rail. Cut the fabric where it meets the leg so that the portion that crosses the leg can be folded under to continue the line of the bottom of the seat rail across the leg. Gimp tacks or small beads of glue can be used to fasten the cover fold across the leg.

Arms and wings that have been covered on the front edge require that the outside cover be smoothed, tightened, and turned under along the front edge (flush with edge or with edge trim, such as welt, brush, or ruching) and blind-stitched in place.

If a panel is to be installed on the front edge of the arm or wing, the front edge of the outside cover is brought around to the front of the arm or wing and tacked where it will be hidden under the panel.

Exposed wood on the front edge requires that the cover be tacked at the rabbet just short of the show wood. If the rabbet is shallow or if there is none and doubling the fabric would make the edge bulky, smear a bead of glue on the cut fabric edge where it will be hidden by the gimp; the glue prevents edge raveling.

The back edge is usually brought around and tacked on the back sides of the posts unless for decorative reasons a border or panel is used along the back edge or the wings and arms are to continue around the post. For back-edge panels or borders, tack the rear edge of arm and wing covers to the outside of the posts inside the eventual border or panel edges. For continuous arms-to-back effects, fold under the rear edge of the cover along the desired seam line, usually the line of the outer edge of the back post. Then blind-stitch the edge to the outside back cover. An alternate method is to pin the arm and back pieces in place, mark the seam locations, remove the pieces, machine-stitch the seams, and then install the piece.

Outside back covers are the last of the major cover pieces to be installed. After installation of edge trim, apply the back cover by the same methods used on arms and wings. Blind-tack or blind-stitch along the top edge. Tack the bottom edge under the seat rail. If side panels will be used on back posts, tack side edges around the back posts. If there will be no post panels, blind-stitch the edges to edge trim. With flow-around arm-to-back or wing-to-back covers, complete outside arm cover installation.

Where blind-stitching is required at the unwelted flow-around arm-to-back seam, use slightly smaller than normal stitches and be extremely careful to produce an even, pull-free seam. Glue or gimp-tack the cover over legs. Install any panels and gimp or double welt that are to cover outer edges.

Dust panels, skirts, and fringes

Dust panels are applied to areas out of sight under the seat and under open arms. Turn the chair upside-down. If welt or brush trim is to be used along the bottom edge and has not already been attached to the cover, attach the welt to the bottom side of the seat rail with cardboard. Cut a piece of cambric 1 inch greater than the bottom of the seat in each dimension. Turn under ¾ inch and slip-tack ¼ inch

Installation of dust panels and bottom welt

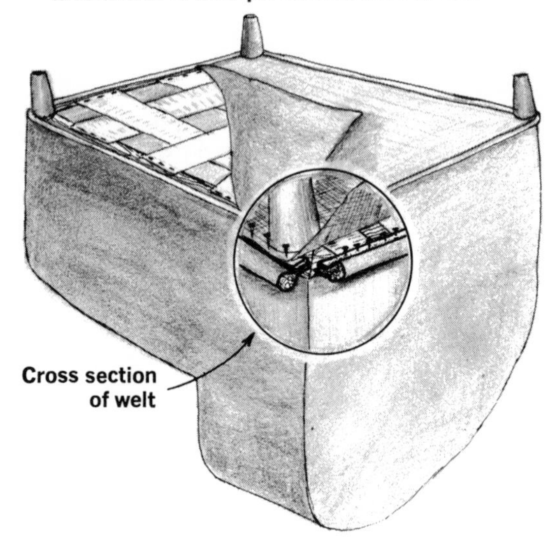

in from the outer edge at the center of the front seat rail. Fold under the other edges and slip-tack at the center of back and side rails. Slip-tack out to the corners, keeping the cambric tight and smooth to prevent any part of it being visible when the chair is upright. Repeat cambric treatment under open arms as needed.

Skirts or bullion fringe are added last. Bullion fringe is blind-stitched to the cover at the bottom edge of the seat rail and should reach to ½ inch from the floor.

Leather and plastic covers

Non-woven, airtight materials such as leather, plastic sheeting, and synthetic leather substitutes fall into an extra-heavy weight category when you compare their handling characteristics with those of other cover materials. It is best to gain skill in using heavy woven fabrics before attempting to use leather and plastic.

Leather. Though leather will stretch, it is difficult to stretch into specific shapes. Leather seldom fits complicated surfaces well, though tufting and channeling pleats in leather will stay neat and smooth once they are formed. Stuffing for leather must be fairly firm, and the shapes must be simple. You can't use a regulator through leather. Standard sewing machine needles work poorly; it is best to use a heavy-duty machine, square pointed leather needles, and polyester thread. Use paraffin wax or silicone slip spray to lubricate the needle, machine foot, and table to prevent the leather from sticking as you sew.

Make layouts for leather covers accurately and preferably at full scale. Mistakes in cutting are very expensive. Leather can be obtained in whole or half hides; their shape and imperfections will probably mean you will have large amounts of waste material. Cut pieces for areas subject to maximum wear from the center of the hide. Stiff leather can be softened somewhat by moistening (not wetting) the back (rough side). Machine-sew leather with a sharp-edged needle and long stitches. Short stitches act like rows of perforations, and the leather will tear along them. Cut welt covers, boxing, and gimp strips as long as possible, to keep piecing to a minimum.

Piece leather by "skiving" the ends of pieces to be joined—cutting the two edges to complementary tapers approximately ½ to ⅝ inch long and joining them. Modern leather worker's contact cement can be used to join the tapered surfaces; on boxing, run two lines of stitches across the joint (see drawing). Place the leather on a smooth surface and then use a very sharp blade to make a slanting cut toward the end from a point ½ inch back from the end. The skived end should be smooth and free of edge fibers.

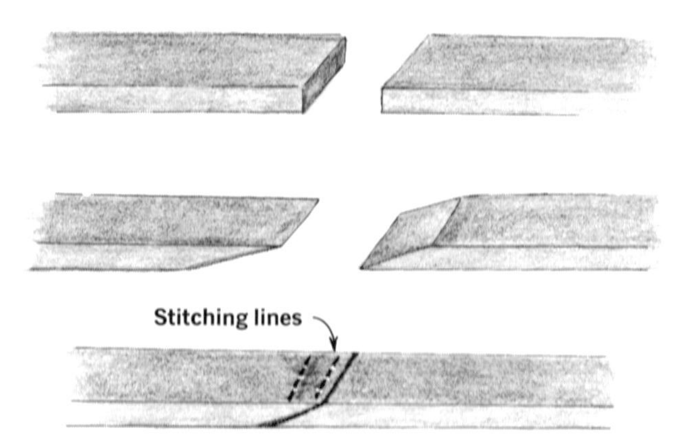

SKIVE AND JOIN leather by slicing at angle, gluing.

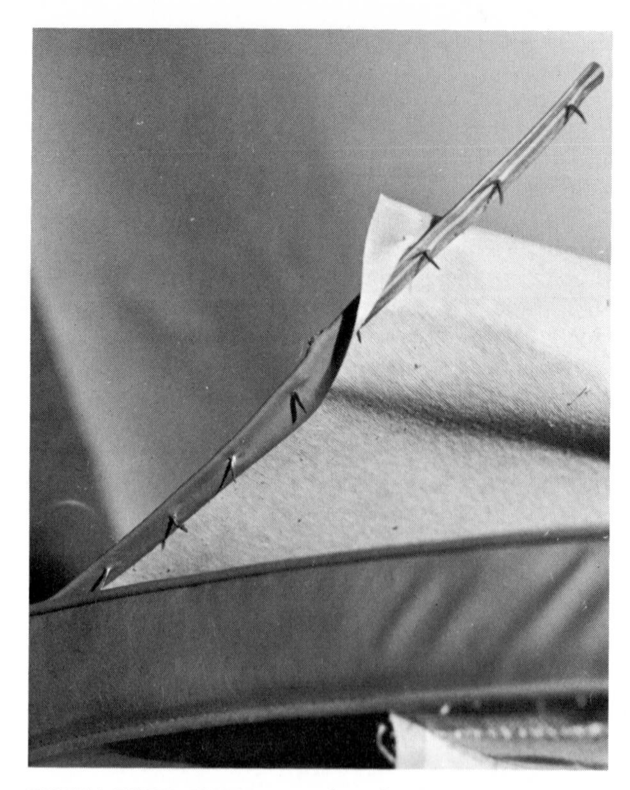
PRETACKED STRIP is used on leather and vinyl outside covers. Mark cover turn-under, then install strip.

Installation of leather inside covers is the same as for fabric, with the exceptions already noted. Outside covers may be handled as fabric, but blind-stitching is difficult and time-consuming. Instead, pretacked metal or cardboard tacking strips are used. Lay the leather on the surface to be covered, mark the exact turn-under point for side seams, remove the leather, and install the pretacked tacking strips. Position the leather on the furniture surface and blind-tack it at the top. Drop the leather forward and align the outer edges of the pretacked strips with the chair edges; drive the tacks in. Use a soft-face mallet or a softwood block under a hammer in order to avoid damage to the leather surface.

Plastic. Leather substitutes of plastic are available both with and without fabric backing. The unsupported material is more prone to tearing and ripping and is seldom used for anything but inexpensive kitchen chairs. Materials with a jersey knit-type backing are more stretchable than those with a felted or hard-weave backing. Handle plastic like leather, but use seams rather than skiving for piecing, punch holes for buttons and at the ends of internal cuts, and use round needles for sewing to minimize tearing.

If you must use unsupported plastic sheeting, use the heaviest gauge material you can. Never use material thinner than 0.012 gauge; this is the minimum gauge for use over springs. Punched holes and the ends of inside cuts should be reinforced with adhesive tape or a dab of vinyl swimming pool repair glue and a piece of muslin or denim. Allow the glue to dry thoroughly before applying any pressure.

Use the largest needle your machine can use and the heaviest cotton or polyester thread the needle can take. Do not make more than 6 stitches per inch. If your machine can't take at least a No. 18 needle, rent a larger machine or have the seams sewn by a professional upholsterer. Use a heat lamp to gently warm and make plastic more flexible for corner shaping and pleating.

SLIP COVERS

Properly fitted slip covers serve many purposes. They protect new or delicate covers for everyday use, hide worn covers, or make possible a seasonal color and style change. You can purchase accent furniture pieces with inexpensive muslin or denim covers, then make several sets of slip covers in different styles and fabrics.

To bring about style changes, you can add or subtract welt lines or add ruching, fringe, or skirts to the slip covers. For instance, a plain spring-edge seat front can be made to look like a banded, boxed, or bordered front by running lines of welt or fringe at appropriate levels across the front of the slip cover.

Choosing and laying out fabric

Most upholstery fabrics are ideal for slip covers. If maximum durability is not required, drapery fabrics may be used. The same color, pattern, and texture guides apply as for regular covers, though you may wish to use less neutral colors, patterns, or textures since they can be changed more easily.

Slip covers may be dry cleaned or laundered, depending on the fabric. If you are planning to launder them, pick a fabric that is washable and colorfast. Always preshrink washable fabrics by soaking them for several hours in cold or tepid water, squeezing dry (don't wring), air drying, and then steam pressing. Many dry cleaners and laundries will shrink material for a small charge per running yard.

Use washable trim or edging for slip covers that will be laundered. Welt has some tendency to pucker when laundered. Edges such as boucle and bullion fringe must be dry cleaned.

Estimate required yardage as you would for regular covers, figuring seam and handling allowances and 4 to 6-inch tuck-in allowances. Extra material may be needed for centering large or prominent patterns on highly visible surfaces. Make a layout to scale and mark cover pieces as described on pages 49 and 51.

When it is necessary to piece fabric across wide seats and backs, do so in line with any cushion divisions and trim the seam with either welt or brush, or make a French seam. Inside back and seat may be covered with a single piece of fabric if enough length is added to allow for a doubled tuck-in between back and seat.

Back and seat sections must have tuck-ins where they meet arms or wings. The tuck-ins are slipped into the crevices between seat and back and between seat and arm. To keep a tuck-in from being pulled out of its crevice, thicken the free edge of the tuck-in. Sew cord, rope, commercial roll edging, cardboard tubes, or even tightly rolled paper into the tuck-in edge—like an oversized self welt (page 50). Never use a rigid material such as a wooden dowel or stiff wire, since the thick edge must be flexible enough to adjust to contours. Without this flexibility the tuck-in or cover would tear when the pull exerted in different places was not equal. Tuck-in allowances for unthickened edges should be 4 inches; for tuck-ins with thickened edges, add three times the diameter of the thickening material plus 1 inch to the basic 4-inch allowance.

Installing the covers

Cut out the slip cover pieces as rectangles. Stretch, smooth, and pin them to the piece of furniture you are covering, in the same order you would use for a final cover. A common order would be seat or platform, arms, wings, backs, skirts, and loose cushions. Inside back and seat are often fitted together.

Work from the center of each edge toward the corners, with seams marked and pinned over the seams of the original cover. Marking seam lines with chalk is helpful. Depending on the shape of the chair, either one or both back post seams should be left open and snap tape, hooks, or zipper installed. Where tuck-ins from adjoining pieces fit into the same crevice, they should be sewn together with a French seam and left unthickened, or the edges should be thickened.

Use the same care in pleating and fitting around curves and obstructions as for regular covers, pinning or basting the material before the final stitching. If the original cover is to be preserved and is of a delicate fabric, be careful that pins go into seams or under welts only. Make fit corrections as you proceed, rather than waiting to do them all at the end.

Stretch, smooth, pin, and mark back and seat pieces along seam lines. Fit around receded arm posts, pleat curves, and miter corners. Mark and pin any boxing, border, or tuck-in places to the top, bottom, and sides of the back and to sides, back, T extensions, and front of the seat. Remove the pieces and machine-sew welt and seams. Trim seam allowances. Stretch, smooth, and pin the assembled cover pieces back in place.

Both arms should be covered at the same time. Fabric pattern or grain should parallel the floor. Pin inside arm pieces in place along seam lines, and make chalk lines where you will sew seams. Pin on any boxing or facing panels and the outside arm covers and mark seam locations. Mark where arm covers contact inside and outside back on adjoining pieces. Remove the cover pieces, sew all welts and seams, join tuck-ins with French seams and add retainers if desired, and trim seam allowances. Stretch, smooth, and pin assembled cover pieces in place.

If there are wing pieces, they are handled the same as arms. Pin inside pieces, any boxing, and outside pieces, marking seam locations and all internal welt lines. Remove and stitch the wing pieces together. Pin in place and mark the seams that will join wings to back and arms on all adjoining pieces. Then remove all cover pieces to be joined together, sew welt and seams, and trim seam allowances. Position assembled cover and pin in place.

Fit the outside back cover using the same methods. (If the inside back has not already been fitted, it must be fitted before the outside back.) When the cover is pinned in place and marked, decide whether it will be necessary to have the back open along one post seam or along both for removing the slip cover. If only one open post seam is needed, remove the covers and welt and sew the top seam, one post seam, and 2 inches down the second post seam; insert snap or Velcro tape (an adhesive fastener), hooks, or zippers the rest of the way. Where both post seams are to be open, sew the top seam and 2 inches down each post seam; then add tapes, hooks, or zippers, following their accompanying instructions. Invisible-type dressmaker's zippers (available up to 24 inches long) are especially good on small, finely woven, lightweight slip covers; when closed they look like regular flat seams.

The bottom edge may be handled in several ways. It can be turned under and hemmed at or just below the bottom edge of the frame. It can be pulled under and around the frame edge and hand-stitched to the cambric or muslin dust cover with running stitches, instead of being tacked to the frame as a regular upholstered cover would be. To add a skirt at the bottom edge, place skirt (see page 48) and cover right sides together with what will be the top of the skirt positioned on the cover at the bottom frame edge location; stitch skirt to cover ½ to ¾ inches above the frame edge location, then drop the skirt forward to hang ½ inch from the floor. Another way to finish the bottom edge is to stitch bullion fringe even with the bottom of the frame so it will hang to within ½ inch of the floor.

Cushion slip covers

Cushion slip covers are made the same as regular cushion covers (see page 66) except that a placket for a zipper or other mechanical closure is located on a hidden edge of the boxing, usually the back or side on seat cushions and the bottom on back cushions.

Often the placket on cushion slip covers is extended 2 or 3 inches around the back corners to make cushion insertion easier. To make this kind of cover, boxing should be cut as long as the combined lengths of the front and both sides, less 4 inches. To make the zipper placket, cut two strips the same width as the boxing and 8 inches longer than the cushion back. If a zipper is to be installed in a double-lap placket (with the edges meeting over the center of the zipper), fold the placket pieces in half lengthwise, center the zipper in the length of the placket, and pin and attach the zipper according to the instructions that come with it. If the zipper or other closure is to be hidden under a single-lap placket, decide how much overlap you want (from ⅜ inch for zippers and snap tape to 1 inch for Velcro tape) and where you want the opening (anywhere from the center of the boxing to one edge, flush with the welt). Fold one piece to serve as the hidden edge of the opening, then fold the other to provide the desired overlap over the first edge. Center the zipper or other closure in the length of the placket and then pin and sew it as directed by the manufacturer.

For zippers with single-lap plackets and for other types of closures, the placket assembly is seamed to the ends of the boxing as if it were a pieced section of the boxing. Double-lap zipper plackets may be seamed to the boxing at the closed end of the zipper but are stitched under a boxing flap at the zipper's open end to provide a cover for the zipper pull tab. Sew plackets to the top and bottom covers as you would attach boxing.

For a more tailored look, you can sew a complete cushion slip cover and blind-stitch the opening shut instead of installing a zipper. Leaving the back welt seam along the bottom cover open, insert the cushion, and then blind-stitch the seam closed.

HOW TO MAKE SLIP COVERS

Making slip covers utilizes many of the techniques familiar to the home seamstress who has made a muslin pattern for a dress. Pieces of fabric are cut slightly oversize and pinned in place, then marked where they will join other pieces. The marked pieces are removed, sewn together along the marked seam lines, and checked for fit. Always check after each seam is sewn; corrections are much easier one seam at a time than if several seams have to be ripped out to reach the original error.

Allow enough fabric for tuck-ins where the back and arms meet the seat. If you forget to allow for tuck-ins, fabric can be sewn on, though the seam will be slightly visible. Add a welt to make the seam look like part of the cover design.

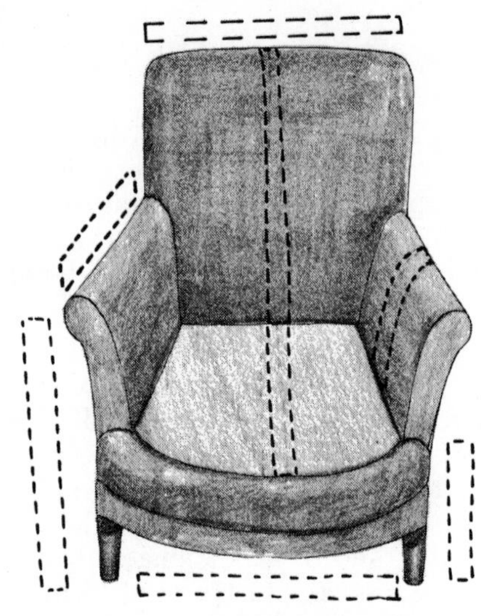

MEASURE the two greatest dimensions for each cover piece. Cut pieces as rectangles, adding seam and tuck-in allowances to measurements you have taken.

CUSHIONS may be covered separately or with seat or back. If you cover over them as part of chair, make cover tight enough to prevent shifting.

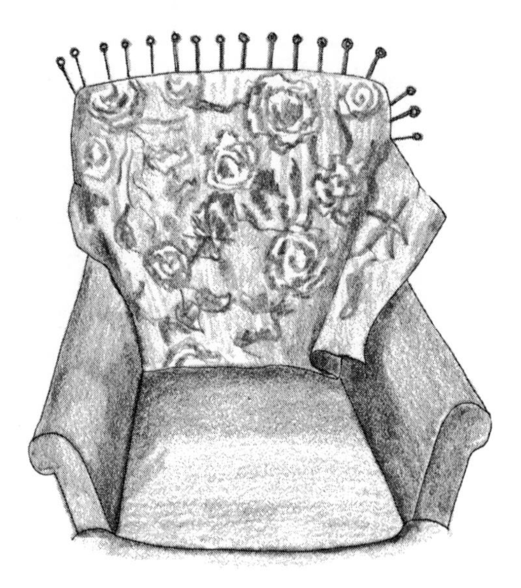

PIN FABRIC rectangles in place; form corner pleats, tuck-ins, seam lines. Pin carefully so original cover won't be damaged. Welts are good pinning points.

MARK PLEATS, tuck-ins, and seam lines with chalk (blackboard-type or tailor's chalk). Fit pieces carefully to avoid puckers or pull marks at seams.

ZIPPERS usually are located in side seams of outside back panel. Zippers should be long enough to clear arm bulges which could hinder installation.

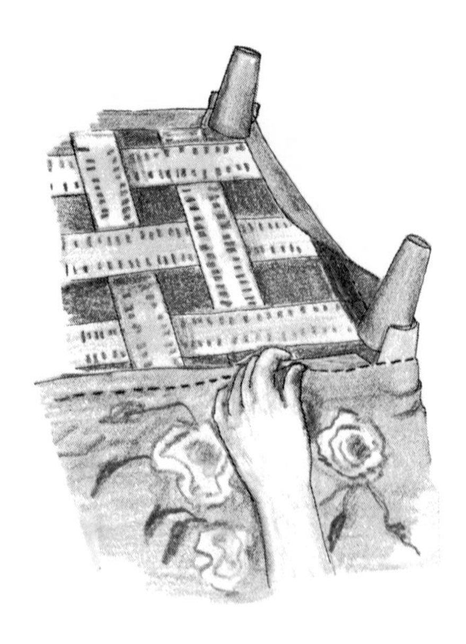

SLIT BOTTOM EDGE at legs. Fold fabric under the rail edge and stitch dust cover to it or tack to rail. Snaps may be used instead of stitching.

ADD A SKIRT and welt by machine-sewing to bottom of assembled slip cover. For trimmer, more permanent finish, use blind-tacking strip at welted seam.

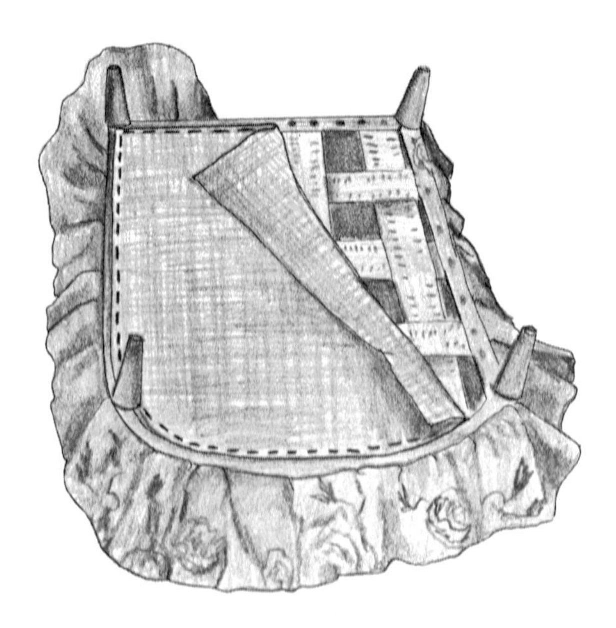

DUST COVER is attached last. Usually it is turned under and stitched to bottom edge of slip cover, but sometimes it is tacked to seat rail over the cover.

Cushions, Pillows, and Bolsters

The three basic types of cushions are fitted loose cushions for supported seats and backs on overstuffed or open frame furniture; throw pillows; and unsupported, shaped, floor or backrest pillows and bolsters.

Any of the materials used for furniture stuffing can be used for cushion stuffing, but some are used more often than others. Fitted seat and back cushions most often have innersprings (Marshall units), rubber or polyurethane foam (alone or over hair or a spring core), down and feathers, felted cotton, or polyester fibers as the principle stuffing. Throw pillows are often stuffed with foam, polyester, down and feathers, kapok, cotton, or even nylon stockings. Oversized floor cushions and unsupported backrest cushions or bolsters are generally somewhat thicker than other types of cushions; the added thickness may be built up around a core of high-density rubberized fiber or foam slab stock, felted sisal, encased and stitched hair, moss, or tow, or even blocks of hard polystyrene insulating foam.

FITTED CUSHIONS

Fitted cushions are made to fit snugly into the seat or back of a piece of furniture. They are completely self-contained, so the cover must fit smoothly—excess material can't be pulled under frame edges. Wait to determine the exact cushion size until all other stuffings and covers (at least muslin covers) that contact the cushion are in place. Don't assume that cushion spaces and shapes that look identical actually are, especially if cushions are to be reversible. Make a pattern for the cushion top, then turn it over so each side is against the opposite arm. If it fits, use the same pattern for both top and bottom cushion covers. If differences show up you will either have to make non-reversible cushions or adjust arms, back, and platform to produce identical arm contours. If the cushions are made non-reversible, the bottom cover can be of decking (see page 56) rather than cover fabric, starting 3 to 4 inches back of the front edge.

Cutting the cover pieces

Rectangles marked cushion top, cushion bottom, cushion boxing, and cushion welting should already be outlined on your upholstery fabric (see pages 48-51). Check to be sure you allowed for handling and seam allowances and then cut out these pieces.

Lay the piece marked "cushion top" right side up on the seat platform. Stretch and smooth the piece out to the platform edges; be sure fabric grain or pattern is correctly aligned and centered, and then use chalk to trace around the outer edge of the open side or sides and the edges contacting arms and back. The chalk line will be the seam line. Remove the piece of fabric from the platform and cut outside the chalk lines, allowing a standard seam allowance (usually 1 inch). You may find it convenient to mark the seam allowance line before cutting.

Place the rectangle marked "cushion bottom" on a flat surface right side up. Lay the cut top piece face down on the bottom piece, align the center fabric grain and pattern, and trace the outline of the top piece on the bottom piece with chalk. Cut along the chalk line on the bottom piece, and then mark the actual seam line 1 inch in from the edge (or whatever seam allowance you are using). An alternate method is to place the bottom rectangle face down on the seat platform and mark the seam line, then add seam allowances and cut.

If you prefer, you can use a paper pattern. This method has several advantages. It gives you a traceable pattern of the actual seam line, the paper pattern is less likely than the actual cover fabric to stretch in use, and the pattern is reusable many times. Place a sheet of heavy brown wrapping paper on the seat platform and mark the edge seams. Cut the paper along the seam line and place on the cover fabric. Trace around the paper, then cut far enough outside this line to leave a standard seam allowance. Be sure to align and center fabric grain and pattern before cutting. If the cushion is not absolutely symmetrical, carefully mark the paper pattern so you know which is the top side.

Boxing is cut across the width of the fabric to match the front edge of the top cushion cover. The measurement across the boxing, from welt to welt, can vary according to furniture style and stuffing material. Some modern pieces have thin cushions with only 2-inch boxing, while others have 6 to 8-inch boxing. Most boxing runs from 2½ inches on puffy, down-filled cushions to 3½ or 4 inches for inner-spring or foam-filled cushions. Leave a seam allowance along each seam edge, where material will be pieced, and at final closing seams. Keep piecing seams out of sight on the back or sides of the finished cushion.

Joining the cover pieces

Sew welting to the seam edge of the top and bottom cushion pieces. (See page 50 for information about welt construction.) The procedure for joining top and bottom pieces to boxing varies slightly, depending on whether you will stuff the cushion by hand or use a machine or hand iron. For a hand-filled cushion, pin the boxing to the center of the top cover front edge, then continue pinning toward and around the corners. Boxing and cover must be equally stretched and smoothed, or wrinkles will result. Machine-sew pinned boxing to top cover, and sew a seam to close boxing where the ends meet

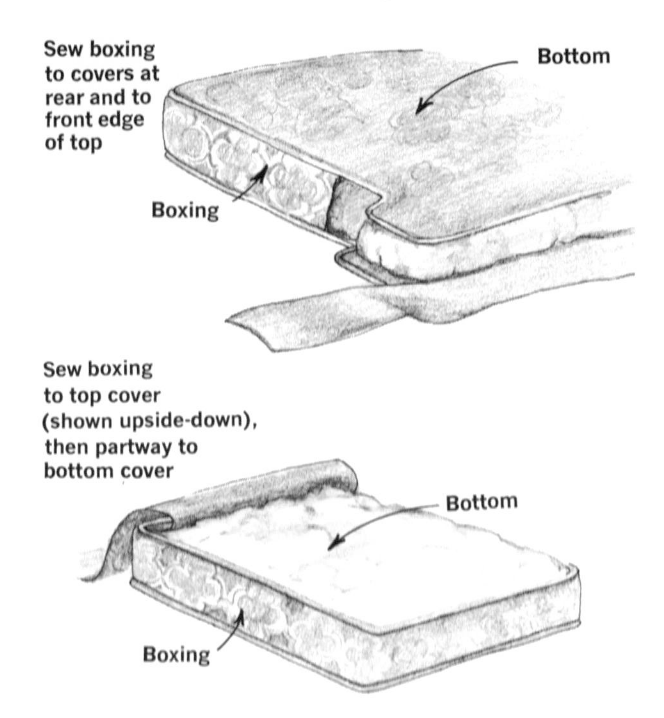

in back (follow single threads across each half to align the seam).

Exactly locate the corners on the top cover, and trace a vertical thread in the boxing strip from each corner to the bottom edge of the boxing; mark the seam allowance at these places. Align the corners of the front of the bottom cover with the corresponding marks on the front boxing edge and pin the welted cover to the boxing. Stretch and smooth cover and boxing equally. Sew the front of the bottom cover to the front of the boxing, leaving sides and back open.

For a cushion to be stuffed by machine or hand iron, leave open only the back or front edge of the boxing, whichever is longer. Always try to leave boxing open in back where practical, but on T cushions a front opening is usually necessary. Arrange piecing of boxing so that it occurs on the sides near the back corner for back filling, or on the sides just back of the T extension for front filling. Sew bottom and top covers to boxing using the same precautions for matching and smoothing as for hand filling.

Muslin cases under final cushion covers are a good idea for the beginner. They provide practice at making a cover without the danger of ruining an expensive piece of fabric. To make one, proceed as for a cover but do not use welt. Because the muslin case will be covered, whip stitches can be used instead of blind stitches.

Stuffing fitted cushions

The choice of stuffings for fitted cushions includes innerspring units (Marshall units), down and feather, polyester fiber, and foam.

Marshall units. Marshall innerspring units are pocketed springs edge-stitched or hog-ringed together (see page 19) in mats shaped to fit inside the cushion. Build the Marshall unit 1 to 3 inches shorter in both front-to-back and side-to-side dimensions than the finished cover, to allow for ½ to 1½ inches of felted cotton between springs and boxing.

Hand-fill a cushion with a Marshall unit by first fitting two or three layers of felted cotton inside the top cover turned upside-down, with enough cotton to extend up the boxing strip. Some upholsterers prefer to tear felted cotton to fit into the top cover only and then tear separate felted cotton strips to fit between springs and boxing. Place a layer of top quality hair stuffing over the cotton. A 2 to 3-inch crowned layer of hair (prepared as described on page 29) is adequate.

Insert the prebuilt springs over the hair. Space springs evenly from side to side, but try to keep between ¾ and 1-inch spacing between springs and the front edge. Take up any front-to-back spacing difference with felted cotton at the back. A front edge too thinly padded soon shows wear or spring marks, while too much padding compacts, interferes with the spring return action, and makes a lumpy front.

Add as many strips of felted cotton between the springs and the cotton already in place at the sides as are necessary to make edges firm (but not so firm as to interfere with spring action). Half or full T cushions which do not have springs in the T extensions will have to be stuffed firmly with cotton.

Build up hair on top of the spring unit the same as beneath it, then tear layers of felted cotton to cover the hair. Use the same number of layers as you used beneath the springs, and tear them so that they meet and fill out the cotton layers against the boxing.

Rubberized hair may be used in place of loose hair if a crown is produced by the concentric layer method described for crowned foam pads (page 35). Medium or soft-density foam may be used in place of loose hair if a thin rubberized or excelsior pad is placed between the inner-spring unit and the foam as a spring insulator.

Pull boxing up straight and smooth, pull the bottom cover back over the felted cotton, pin it to the boxing at corner marks, and then pin all edges to be sewn. Check to make sure there are no wrinkles, lumps, or inadequately filled areas. Open pinned edges as necessary to make adjustments. Use a regulator or a stuffing bar to place additional cotton under existing top layers to fill voids.

Apply a cushion stretcher (see photos) to one of the side seams, adjust pins as needed for a smooth seam, and blind-stitch boxing to the welt on the bottom cover along the stretched side, stopping just short of the back corner. Do the same on the other side but do not stitch the back seam until you have shaped the cushion.

With the cushion on a solid surface, work the stuffing toward the front edge. With most fabrics you can do this by going over the cover from front to back welt with a sharp slapping-brushing motion. Do this to all surfaces to compact the cotton and show up any lumps or voids. Break up lumps by unpinning the back edge and adjusting under the cotton layers with a regulator or stuffing bar. Fill voids by folding a piece of cotton over a regulator, your fingers, or a stuffing bar, then sliding it into position under the cotton layers. Check carefully at front corners and T extensions and along the back edge; any stuffing weakness at these points creates floppy corners and wrinkles. When stuffing is adjusted, align back cover corners and boxing, stretch and smooth the fabric, and blind-stitch back boxing to bottom cover.

For machine or hand iron filling, build cotton and hair layers into hand irons or machine box preset to the pillow size. Close the iron or machine and slip the open end of the cover tautly over the box as far as it will go (see photos on next page). Disassemble and withdraw the hand iron or actuate foot-operated plunger on the machine to push the filler out of the box into the cover. Adjust stuffing and sew seams as for a hand-filled cushion.

Down and feather stuffing. Cushions filled with down and feathers always need a ticking case to

STRETCH CUSHION seams when hand-stitching to ensure correct alignment and reduce puckering. Twine and skewers are being used to stretch and align seam at left; commercial stretcher is shown at right.

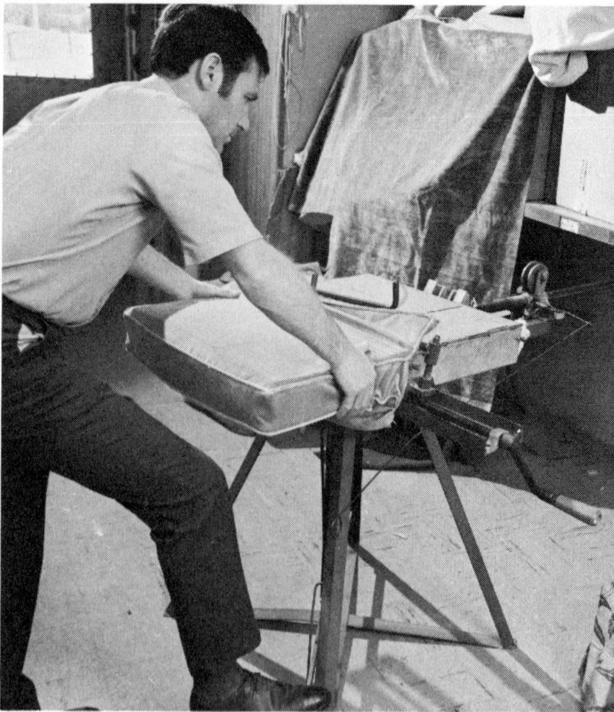

BUILD CUSHION FILLING into metal machine box, close box to cushion size, slide cover over, and eject stuffing into cover by operating foot pedal. Hand iron is a similar metal box without mechanical aids.

keep down from coming through the final covers. The ticking case is made larger than the cover to ensure fullness; add 1 inch to the length and width for pillows up to 12 inches square, and add ⅛ inch for each additional 6 inches of length or width.

Ticking cases for cushions 12 by 12 inches or smaller often are made as single compartments the same shape as the cover, but larger. Cases for larger cushions are made with tube-shaped compartments that run from side to side of the piece of furniture to combat the tendency of down to settle to the bottom of back cushions and to the back of seat cushions. For best results, the compartments should not be wider than 8 inches. Usually a cushion is divided into three compartments, but more should be used if the cushion is long or if severe shifting can be expected in a given situation.

Use downproof ticking to make the casing. Cut top and bottom pieces to the shape and size of the final cover plus the fullness allowance and seam allowances. Cut boxing the same size as cover boxing. Welt is not used on casing. The ticking strips for the compartment dividers should be the same width as the boxing at the ends, curving out on both edges so the strip is twice the height of the boxing at 5 to 6 inches from the end. Some upholsterers make one edge of the divider straight, but divider strips that curve out on both top and bottom edges provide a more wrinkle-free casing, especially under thin covers.

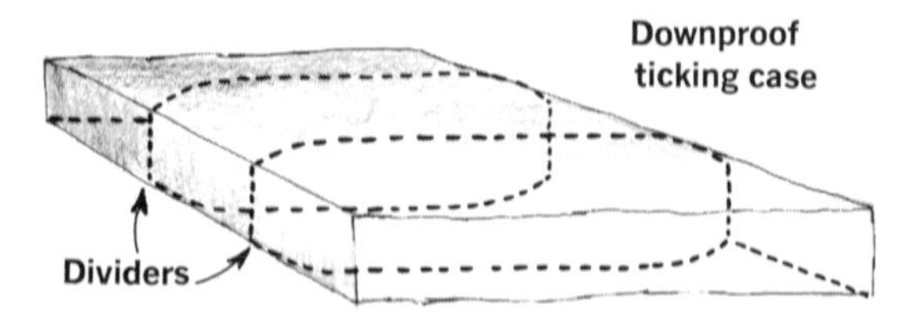

Sew ticking case boxing to the casing bottom piece all the way around. Sew compartment dividers to casing bottom and boxing, using regular flat seams. Sew dividers to casing top, starting at the center divider; then sew the top to the top edge of the boxing on three sides, leaving one side that opens to all the compartments unsewn. Stuff compartments uniformly by hand or vacuum cleaner (see photo on next page). When resiliency seems right, pin cover closed, use slapping and beating motions to evenly distribute the down, and then sit on the cushion to make sure it does not feel hard or lumpy. The cushion should rise back to shape without depressed areas, but without the tautness of spring or foam cushions.

Prepare the cushion cover as you would for a spring-filled cushion. Stuff the filled casing into the cover, stretch the cover, smooth it, and sew it shut.

Kapok or polyester stuffing. If kapok or polyester fiber stuffing is used, it should be muslin-encased before it is put into cushions. Make a muslin case

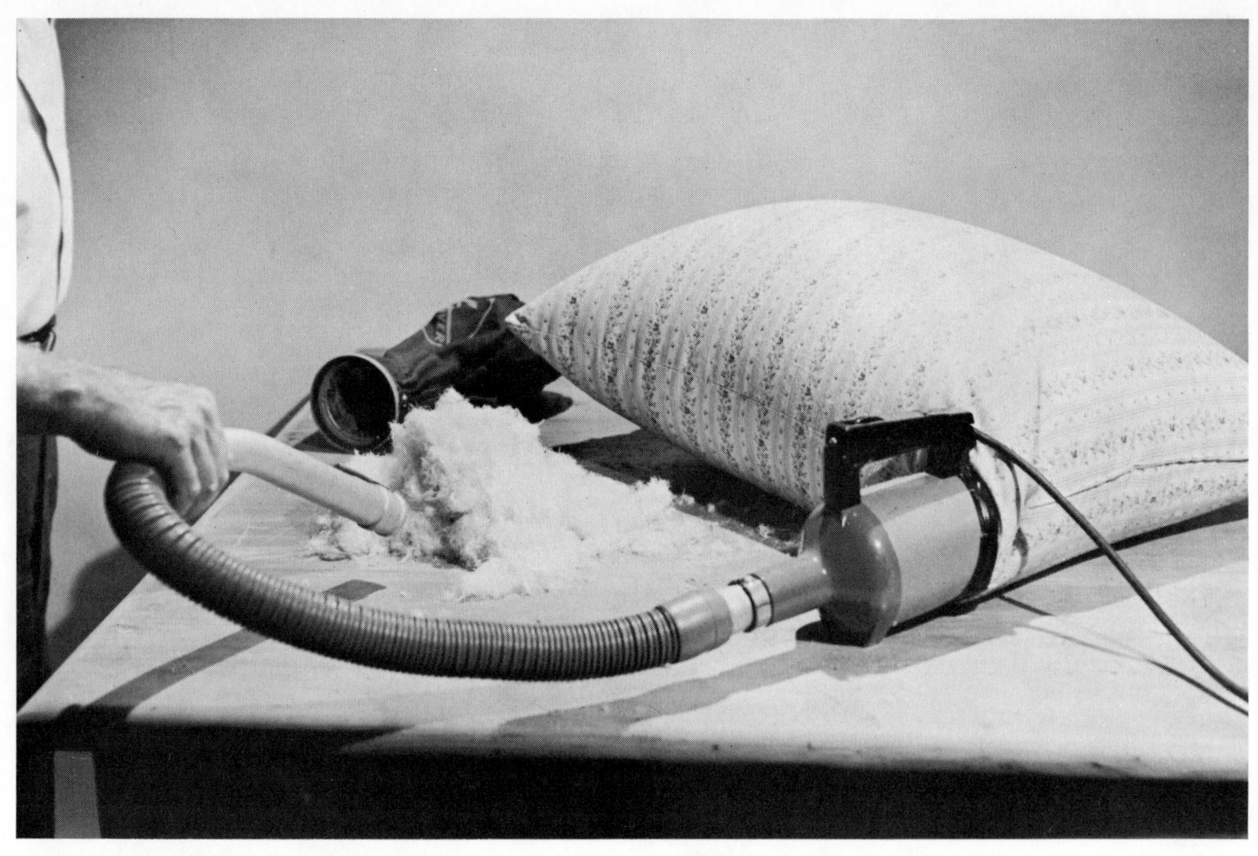

DOWN CUSHIONS can be filled by taping seam opening over outlet of direct-flow vacuum cleaner and using cushion as dust bag. Small units need slow feed to prevent clogging; large ones work faster.

the same way as you would make a ticking case for down pillows. Compartments are often omitted on commercially-made cushions, but for best results they should be used.

Foam stuffing. Covers for cushions stuffed with rubber and polyurethane foam are constructed exactly as those for innerspring units. Depending on the style of the piece of furniture, boxing can range from 2 to 8 inches from welt to welt. Crowns may or may not be used with rubber or polyurethane foam stuffing. One way to produce reversible cushions with crowns on both sides is to build up concentric layers of foam. Two other methods utilize single slabs the same thickness as you want the crown to be. All three methods are discussed below.

If you build the crown with concentric foam layers, a 1-inch border slab is used, so the top and bottom pieces will have to be cut slightly smaller than the finished cushion filler to prevent the foam from being over-compressed and straining the cover. Two inner cores are cut the same shape as the top and bottom, but the first is 4 inches smaller in length and width than the top and the second is 4 inches smaller than the first. Center and cement (see page 34) the inner cores to the top slab to produce a low, stepped pyramid with 2-inch step widths all around. Center the bottom slab and cement it to the cores; do not cement the 2-inch lips of the top and bottom slabs together.

STEPPED FOAM is base for crowned cushion.

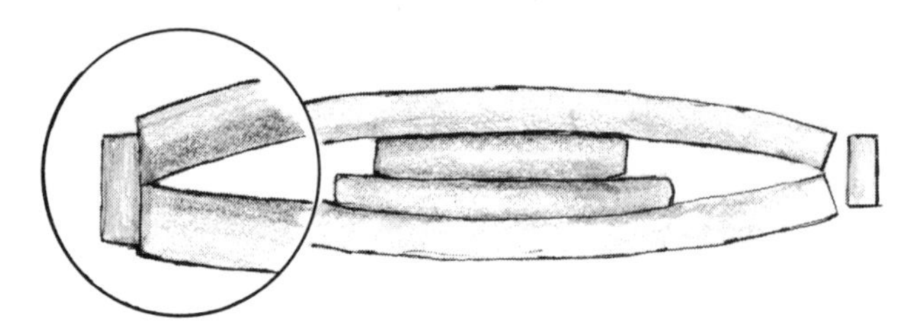

BOXING SLABS are glued to edges of crowned cushion.

Cut border or boxing slab for each edge the same length as the corresponding edge of the unbordered cushion and the exact height of the cover boxing from welt to welt; the boxing will be from ½ to 1½ inches narrower than the foam edge to which it is to be glued. Apply cement to one side of the border and to the outer edges of the top and bottom slabs and allow it to become tacky. Center the border between the top and bottom of the outer slabs (do not overlap border pieces at the ends) and glue in place. This will leave a ledge on all four sides of each border when all the border pieces are installed. When the cement holding the borders to the cushion slabs is firm, apply cement to both faces of each ledge, allow it to become tacky, and then press the pieces together to form rounded edges and corners.

Allow the cement to dry for at least four hours before trying to stuff the foam into a muslin case or final cover. Otherwise areas softened by the cement solvents could tear.

To make a crowned cushion from a slab of foam the same thickness as the crown, draw lines half the cover boxing height from the top and bottom edges on all sides to be crowned. For a 5-inch slab to be used with 3-inch boxing, you will have lines drawn 1½ inches from the top edge and 1½ inches from the bottom edge with a 2-inch space between. Use an electric meat-carving knife or a serrated-edge bread knife to slice out a wedge between the two lines.

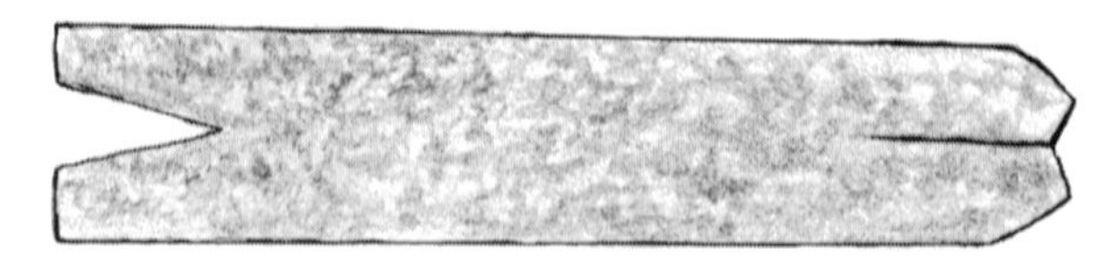

CUT OUT WEDGE and glue inner surfaces together.

The depth of the wedge will determine the slope of the crown. The deeper the wedge, the shallower the crown slope will be; the shorter the wedge, the more abrupt the crown edge will be. Do not try to cut away the whole amount in one slice, or you will overcompress the foam and distort the cut. Instead, make several shallow cuts. Do not cut all the way to the center of the slab.

Apply cement to the two inner surfaces created by cutting out the wedge, allow it to dry until it is tacky, and then pinch the surfaces together. If the edge is objectionably ridged, slice it off and cement on a slab of soft-density 1-inch foam stock cut to the exact boxing height.

Another way to make a crowned cushion is to use three slabs of stock, the two outer ones of soft-density foam and the inner one of medium-density foam. The medium-density slab should match the boxing height, and the soft layers should each be one half the difference between the boxing and crown heights. Some suppliers have layered stock available, but you will usually have to make your own. Simply cement the three layers together. The soft layers usually compress sufficiently at the edges to form a crown when covered. Sometimes they may have to be shaped with scissors to give the shape you want.

If velvet or other pile fabric is used as a cushion cover, muslin casing must be used between the foam and the cover or the foam will pull the pile fibers through the backing. Muslin casing is useful for any foam-filled cushions, since it helps the filling slide easily into the final covers without the friction common to foam. Make muslin casing the same size as the final covers.

If foam is to be placed into covers without muslin, use cotton fiber or polyester fiber top stuffing or sprinkle foam surfaces and filling tools with talcum powder to minimize friction. Felted cotton or polyester over either plain or muslin-cased foam will make the cushion less rubbery. These fibers, especially polyester, are often used over flat cushions to produce a puffy crown. To crown a cushion in this way, tear sheets of cotton or polyester into concentric layers for both top and bottom and then wrap the entire cushion with a layer of cotton or polyester.

TOP AND BOTTOM are soft foam; center is medium-density. Soft foam will compress at edges to form crown.

THROW PILLOWS

Almost all types of cushion stuffings can be used for throw pillows, though innerspring units are seldom used. Some pillows are even stuffed with nylon stockings or foam chips; neither of these holds up well under hard wear, however.

Boxed-edge pillows are built the same way as fitted furniture cushions, except that they seldom have to exactly fit a given space.

Covers for single-welt pillows with either knife edge or rounded edge are measured as shown on page 49. On single-welt pillows the corners will be pulled to less than right angles by the stuffing, which is thickest at the center. If you want fully right-angled corners, cut covers normally, sew and stuff them, then pin the corners straight. Remove the stuffing, resew the pillows as pinned, and restuff. If this is first done in a muslin casing, the muslin can be used as the pattern for the final cover.

LARGE PILLOWS AND BOLSTERS

Large floor seating cushions can be built over a central frame like a hassock, with a core of coarse fiber first stuffing for shaping, or with many layers of second or top stuffing materials. The drawings on this page show some examples. Covers over framed hassock units are made like seat covers, and covers for unframed units are made like cushion and pillow covers.

Bolsters may be shaped by the same method as large floor seating pillows, but since they are used on furniture or beds they should be kept as light as possible for easy lifting and handling. A bed backrest with arms could have its basic shape formed in either of two ways: You could stuff a sewn-to-shape cover and rely on the cover to hold the shape, or you could shape a fairly stiff core and cover it with foam or other second and top stuffing materials. For the first method, cut and sew the cover, leaving the bottom or back open. Then place several layers of cotton or polyester against the inside of the cover. Stuff the remaining space tightly with felted cotton or coarser fibers such as excelsior. When the stuffing is sufficiently hard-packed, cover the back with a layer of cotton and sew the cover closed.

For the second method, build a shaped core by stitching or cementing together layers of hard-density rubberized fiber or foam or felted excelsior or other coarse fiber, or make a core out of the type of stiff insulating foam used for instrument and typewriter shipping cases and picnic coolers. The drawing below shows one possible way to cut the foam.

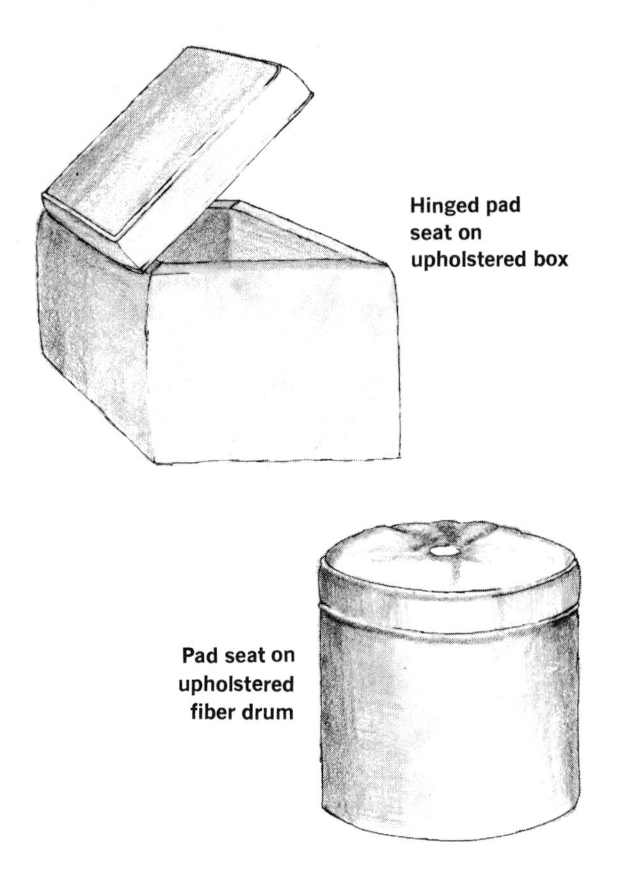

Hinged pad seat on upholstered box

Pad seat on upholstered fiber drum

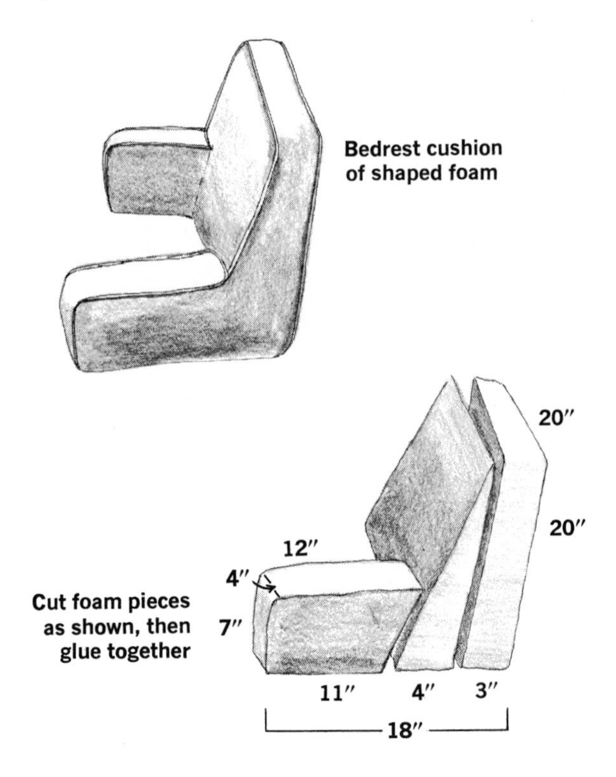

Bedrest cushion of shaped foam

Cut foam pieces as shown, then glue together

Cover the core with soft foam, felted cotton, or polyester, and then make the final cover as you would for a cushion. Backrest arms will require measuring and cutting covers much as you would for continuous back and arms on a chair; all edges will be stitched instead of tacked, unless you use a wooden base.

LAWN AND PATIO FURNITURE

All outdoor furniture can be covered with loose cushions over webbing. Cushions may be knife-edged or boxed, and they should be of as durable and weather-resistant a fabric as you can find. Suitable fabrics include sail-making materials and ducks, twills, and light-weight canvases of the type used for tents and awnings. Trim such as sunfast, preshrunk brush edging, or welt is needed to camouflage seam pucker caused by normal all-weather use. If you prefer a plastic-coated, waterproof material, choose one that is designed for sun and weather exposure.

Polyurethane foam, polyester, and kapok are usually used to stuff outdoor furniture. Most other fibers are too susceptible to water damage; foam rubber is comfortable but expensive for the short life of most outdoor cushions. Polyurethane foam gives best results if wrapped in a layer or two of polyester batting, both to protect the foam from the sun and to produce the desired puffiness.

Large cushions such as those for sun lounges should be loosely tufted or surface buttoned. Use a button on each side of every point, use a slip knot to pull the stuffing down to the desired height, and add an overhand knot over the slip knot.

Standard woven, plastic tape webbing for outdoor furniture is available at most large drug, variety, hardware, and department stores. Look for webbing with a specific life guarantee; standard tape seldom lasts more than one full year in strong sun. Attach the webbing like webbing for regular upholstered furniture, using tacks or staples for wooden frames and screws for metal frames. More hand stretching is needed than for regular upholstery; don't use a spiked stretcher, though one of the other types shown on page 10 could be used on wooden frames.

The plastic-covered wire or rope wrapped across the small frame dimension on some outdoor furniture usually lasts longer than tape webbing. To replace it, wind plastic-covered wire or rope clothesline, nylon or polyester rope, or replacement material from the manufacturer around the frame. Do not remove all the old material before starting to wind the new material—you may need a reference to duplicate the original winding. The line is usually looped around pegs or raised rivets on the bottom side of the frame and then brought back up over the top of the rail.

An alternative to tape or rope webbing on an open frame is laced canvas. Use heavy tent, awning, or sailmaker's fabric; some of the new polyester canvases wear especially well. Machine-hem the edges and install grommets, and then lace the canvas to the frame. Heavy wire or metal rods can be sewn into the canvas edges to reinforce them. The lacing is then threaded through slits, button holes, or grommets in the canvas, with the rod between the edge and the grommets. Aluminum or plastic-coated steel rods can be used, but avoid any material that will corrode and stain canvas.

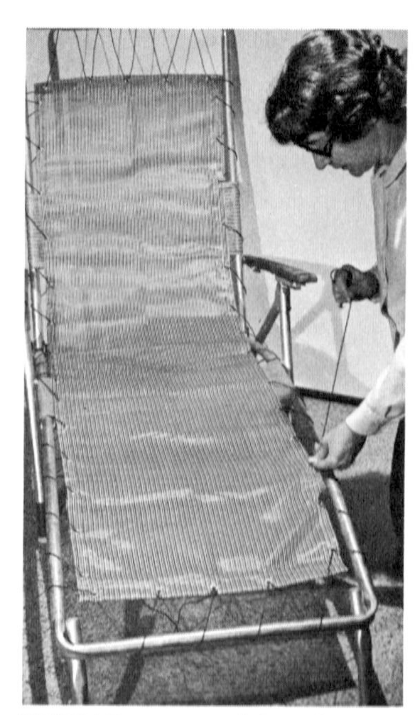

THREAD strong cord through grommets in edge of fabric; use a whipstitch pattern to wind around frame.

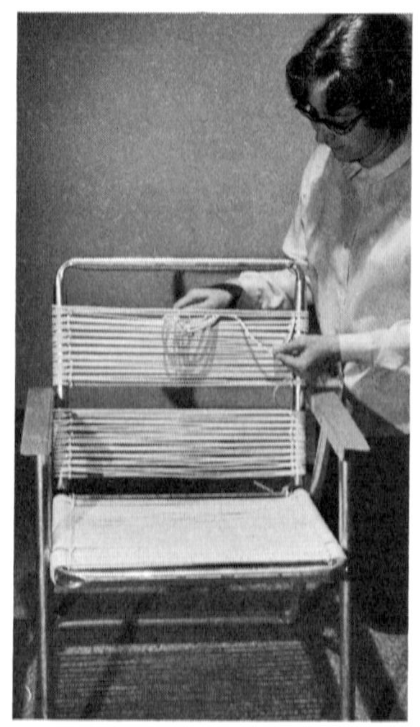

WIND plastic clothesline across frame opening in an over-and-under pattern or in the pattern shown.

FOLD plastic webbing end to a point; insert retaining screw in center of triangle formed, folds on outside.

Caning and Rushing

Caning is the process of weaving rattan cane strips through holes in a frame edge or wedging prewoven cane webbing in grooves cut into a frame. Rushing is the process of weaving natural rush or a substitute around the outer edges of a frame. Caning is most often associated with intricately styled chairs, while rushing is most often found on less formal stools. Both are also attractive when used as panels on walls, doors, and cabinets.

Cane is the thin, hard, glossy bark of a rattan palm cut into narrow, 6 to 10-foot-long strips. These are woven into lightweight panels, usually in an openwork pattern. An average caned seat panel requires 2 to 2½ ounces of cane.

Natural rush is made of the twisted dry leaves of several wet-land plants, including cattails, flag, and bulrush. Because natural rush leaves are short and must be twisted together to make weavable lengths, fiber paper and ropelike substitutes are widely used. Reed (made of split rattan cane) and splints (thin strips of hickory or ash) are natural materials often woven in the same patterns as rush.

CANE WEAVING

Cane chair seats can be made in two ways—by weaving individual strands by hand through holes in the frame, and by using prewoven (usually machine-woven) caning webs. Prewoven caning is held in place by splines—strips of hickory or rattan—driven into routed grooves in the frame. Only a few simple tools are needed for recaning by either method. Hand caning requires an awl or scribe, a pair of scissors, a sharp knife, a ruler, a pair of draftsman's dividers (available at art supply stores), a half dozen wooden pegs (either golf tees or pegs whittled from ¼-inch dowels), and a caning needle (see page 76). To use prewoven cane webbing you will need a small mallet, a chisel, scissors, and a small assortment of hardwood spline-driving wedges.

Prewoven cane webbing

Machine-made cane webbing can be ordered through upholstery shops in various widths, usually from 8 to 18 inches and sometimes 20, 22, 30, and 36 inches, and in any reasonable length and desired pattern. If you are recaning a seat, it will be helpful if you take along a piece of the old caning when you order new caning. To find out where you can buy cane webbing, look in the yellow pages of the phone book under "Chair Caning."

Soak cane webbing in hot to near boiling water for several minutes, until it is thoroughly pliable. Remove it from the water and place it on the seat while it is still damp. Center the cane webbing over the seat, being certain that it extends ½ inch beyond the spline groove on all sides and that the weave parallels the line joining the tops of the front legs. Cut the webbing ½ inch outside the spline groove all the way around. Begin along the front and drive the webbing into the groove with mallet and hardwood wedge; then wedge it into the groove on the back and finally on the sides. Set the cutting edge of a chisel against the cane at the bottom outer corner of the groove and strike the chisel butt with a mallet just hard enough to cut the cane (see drawing). Repeat all along the groove.

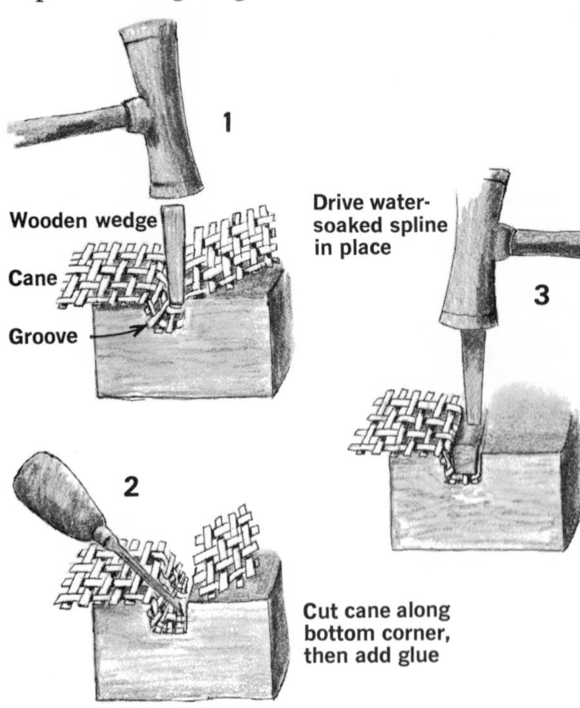

Put enough glue into the groove so some will be squeezed out when the spline is inserted; use any good woodworking glue, such as hot or liquid hide, casein, urea, or a good white glue. Soak the spline in hot water until it is thoroughly pliable, then place it over the groove and drive it into place with a soft-faced mallet and wooden wedges. On a one-piece spline circling the seat, join the ends at the rear of the seat. Where groove corners are sharp angles, use separate spline strips for each side and miter them at the corners. When the spline is driven in all the way, it should be almost flush to the cane. Sponge off excess glue. Allow cane and spline to dry; the cane will shrink enough to become taut and smooth.

The hairlike fuzz on the cane seat can be removed by sanding very carefully with sandpaper or by singeing with a soft blue flame produced by a gas stove or propane torch. Be careful not to scorch the cane; moisten the cane, use the coolest (most noiseless) blue flame you can produce with your torch, and move the flame over the cane quickly enough to singe the fuzz without changing the cane color. The flame must be clean and blue—any yellow will smoke the cane.

Cane will normally dry to a glossy finish if the outer side was kept uppermost while weaving. Additional gloss or surface protection may be added by coating the seat with shellac, lacquer, or varnish after the cane is thoroughly dry.

Furniture, door panels, walls, and mirror or picture frames can all be decorated by applying cane webbing to the surfaces. Staple, glue, and trim as shown in the photographs on page 77.

Hand caning

Hand-caned chair panels are made by weaving individual strands of cane in a pattern and passing the strands through holes in the frame edges. Hole size and spacing depends on the size of the cane used. If you are recaning a seat, check hole size and spacing to determine the largest size you can use. Smaller cane or two sizes of cane may be used for more delicate or elaborate weaves.

Cane Size	Hole Diameter	Hole Spacing
Carriage and Superfine	⅛ inch	⅜ inch
Fine-Fine	3/16 inch	½ inch
Fine	3/16 inch	⅝ inch
Medium	¼ inch	¾ inch

The photographs show the steps toward making the standard six-strand or octagonal weave. Place all the cane strips in water to soften; in cold water the

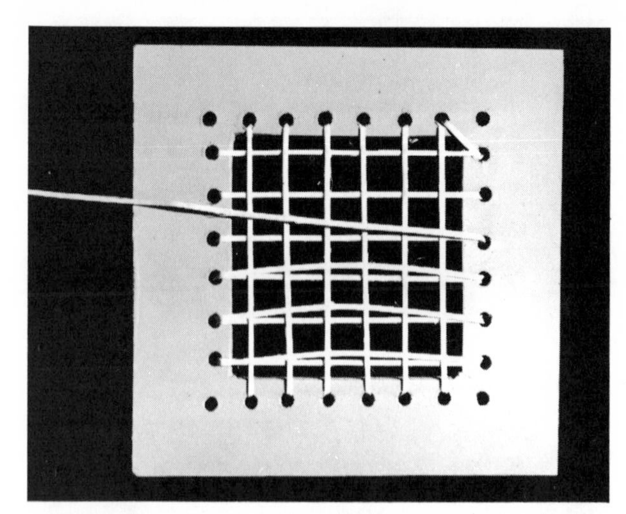

WEAVE layer of horizontal and vertical strands, then add second horizontals on other side of verticals.

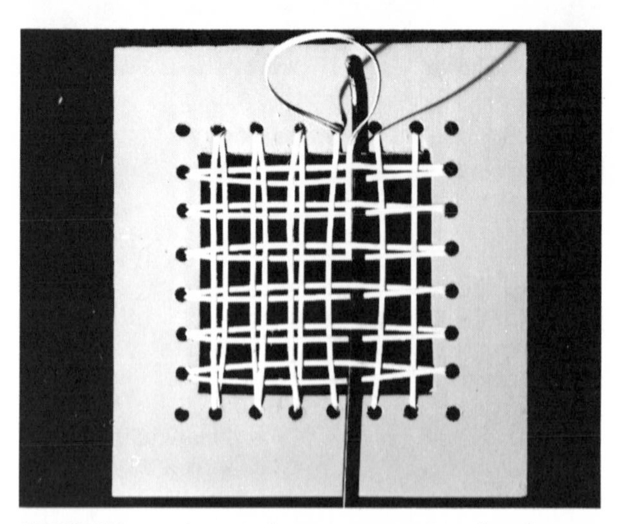

SECOND set of verticals goes over and under alternate horizontal strands. Blunt wire bodkin separates strands.

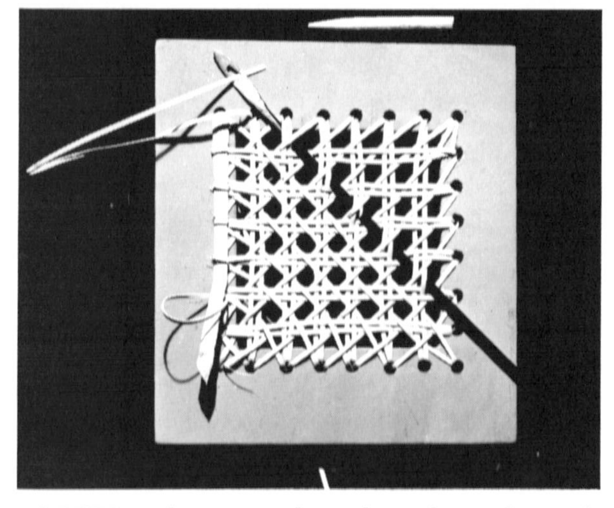

BODKIN with eye, used to draw diagonal strands through, is heavy hanger wire, flattened and drilled.

START RUSHING at corner; continue counter-clockwise with incomplete figure eights across corners.

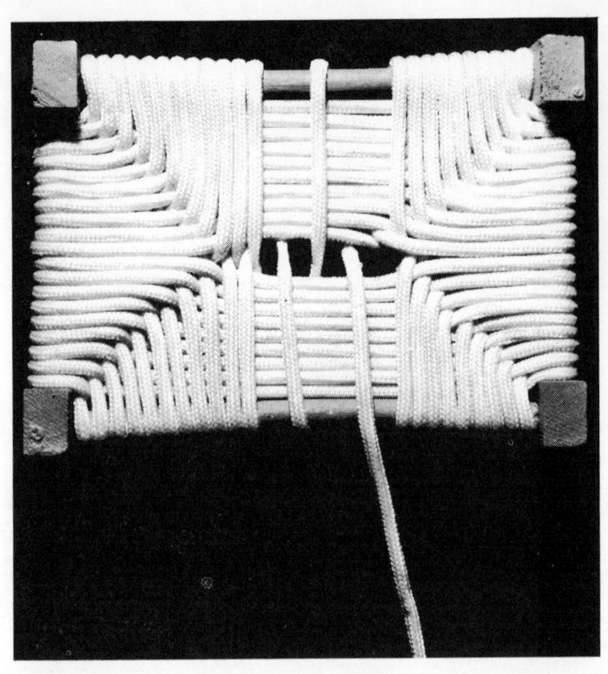

FILL CENTER of long dimension by weaving figure eights after short dimension has been filled in.

strips may take an hour or more to reach maximum pliability, but hot water reduces soaking time to minutes. When the cane is thoroughly pliable, remove a single strand from the water (the remainder can stay in the water until needed) and start weaving by inserting (from the top) 3 inches of the cane through a corner hole. (On non-rectangular frames, start with the center strands of horizontal and vertical rows and the corner-to-corner diagonals, then work out from each central strand toward each side.) Wedge the cane in place with a golf tee or other wooden peg. After weaving the first several strands, remove the wooden peg and tie the loose starting end to an adjoining segment, using a single overhand knot, or coil the end two or three times around the adjoining segment and press flat. New cane strands can be tied in the same way. Make all knots on the back side of the work under the frame edge.

The bodkins or weaving needles shown were made from lengths of extra-heavy coat hanger wire. One is a blunt wire with a slight bend ½ inch from the working end; it is used to separate the cane strands and guide the weaving cane. The other has a flattened and curved head with a hole or eye and is used to thread cane through the weave (this needle is available at upholsterers' supply shops).

A strip of cane wide enough to cover the holes may be added at the frame edges to protect the cane from excessive wear. The edging strip is cut ½ inch longer than the distance between end holes on each side, and ¼ inch of each end is tapered and pushed down into the end hole. The smallest cane used in the weave is used to form loops up through the holes (often every other hole) to hold the strip in place. Sand or burn off the fuzz and finish as desired.

RUSHING

Natural rush is seldom used today for seat weaving because it is hard to handle and the leaves must be soaked and twisted together to make weavable lengths. Rush substitutes are available in continuous lengths. Paper twist and other natural or synthetic fiber rushing is available in seat-length spools, balls, or hanks from upholstery suppliers and mail order woodworker's supply houses. The tougher types of ordinary string or small ropes are often used for rushing. Even cane is woven in rush patterns.

The photographs show the steps to weaving the traditional X-pattern. The weave should be stuffed between bottom and middle layers of the weave (there are three layers) to provide the smooth, filled-out look associated with this weave. Use scraps of the weaving material or twists of brown paper for the stuffing. A stuffing bar or stick is handy for inserting stuffing.

Tacks may be used on the underside of the frame to secure or position strands. Use a dull knife blade, screw driver, or stuffing regulator to position the strands.

DECORATING WITH PREWOVEN CANE

Machine-woven cane webbing is ideally suited for a wide variety of do-it-yourself projects. You can use it to give a new look to old furniture, add textural interest to a surface, and screen or ventilate an area.

The handsome chest of drawers shown in the photograph below was completely transformed by the addition of cane facing. The chest was professionally stripped of several layers of paint, sanded, and given three coats of stain (it was buffed between coats) and two coats of sealer. Then cane was stapled to front and side surfaces, and molding (½-inch on drawers, ¾-inch on sides) was nailed on. It is a good idea to use white glue as well as staples when you put on the caning.

Cane panels are good for providing air circulation inside a closet. Cut out center sections from the door (leave crosspieces) and cover with a long piece of caning. Trim with molding. Prewoven caning also makes attractive cabinet doors, clothes hampers, indoor containers for potted plants, and stools. Stapled to a piece of plywood and trimmed with molding, it is a good backing on which to mount a mirror with clips.

CUT CANING to size, soak in water, let drip a few minutes, and staple on.

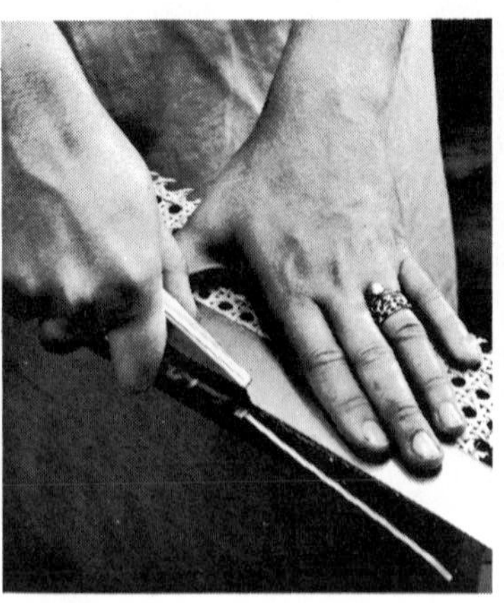

TRIM with knife along straight edge. Add more staples if needed.

NAIL on molding, covering staples. Countersink nails, fill with putty.

EYECATCHING chest of drawers has completely new look with addition of cane facing, molding trim.

Some Common Upholstery Terms

Band. The fabric strip used around the edge of spring-edge and platform spring construction. The top edge of the band is hand-sewn to the edge wire and the bottom edge tacked to the frame. (See text on page 53, sketch on page 56.)

Blind. Out of sight or hidden, as in blind-tacking (sketch, page 23), stitching (sketch, page 53), or doweling (text, page 5), where the tacks, stitches, or dowels are deliberately hidden from view.

Boucle Edging. A glossy edging of looped strands used to emphasize seams and outlines.

Border. A fabric strip blind-tacked at the top edge and tacked at the bottom to the frame, as below a band. (See text on page 53, sketch on page 56.)

Boxing. A strip of fabric that forms the thin edge of a cushion. (See text on page 53, sketch on page 67.)

Braces. Frame members which run between front and back seat rails to provide support on wide seats and occasionally to serve as pull-through slats and attaching points for seat covers. (See sketch on page 7.)

Bullion Fringe. A fringe of single or looped cords used as a skirt at the base of some upholstered furniture. Often very ornate with a high gloss finish.

Buttoning. The use of buttons to hold final cover and stuffing in place and to provide a low relief decorative effect. Not to be confused with tufting.

Cable Springs. Originally oversized rubber bands, now most often loops of thin close-wound coil springs encased in plastic tubing. Used in Scandinavian furniture. (See text on page 22.)

Caning. The process of weaving thin strips of the center layer of rattan cane for use as seat and decorative panels. Also, the woven strips. (See text on page 75.)

Cased Understuffing. Coarse stuffing material covered or encased in burlap and used to fill out a shape, usually on a top rail or arm board. Actually a rounded version of a large stitched-edge roll. (See sketch, page 27.)

Chamfer. A bevel or sloped edge. Also, to produce a bevel edge.

Channeling. Enclosing stuffing in fabric tubes or channels to provide a strongly linear decoration in the form of rounded ridges with sharply defined pleated depressions between them. (See text, sketch on page 38.)

Chipboard. A tough, hard cardboard, used by upholsterers as tacking strips and sheet webbing where normal webbing strength is unnecessary.

Coil Springs. Spirals of steel wire which provide the major elasticity in upholstered furniture. (See text on page 13, photos on page 14.)

Cores. Cylindrical holes molded into foam rubber to reduce weight and improve resiliency. Older-style foam has cores 1 inch or larger in diameter, but modern pin cores seldom exceed ¼ inch in diameter.

Decking. Any fabric used as a substitute for expensive cover fabrics on cushion-supporting platforms or decks which will be hidden by the cushions. Usually denim or any of several brush-finished fabrics sold for this purpose.

Dowel. A round hardwood peg used to join pieces of wood.

Dust Cover. Fabric tacked or stitched to the underside of an upholstered frame to prevent particles of upholstery materials from falling out onto the floor. Usually a stiff black cambric is used. (See sketch on page 60.)

Edge Rolls. Fiber-filled fabric tubes with roughly round or triangular-shaped cross sections, used to soften frame, platform, and spring edges. (See text on page 24, sketches and photos on pages 24, 25, 26.)

Felted Stuffing. Fiber stuffing matted into sheets, usually by rolling it under pressure. Most often the term refers to cotton or polyester batting used for top padding, but it also includes coarser fiber sheets.

Fiber Stuffing. Stuffing material that consists of filaments or threadlike particles .(See text on page 28.)

French Back. An upholstered open back, found on many side or occasional chairs, which resembles a round or oval picture frame with an upholstered center.

French Seam. The upholsterers' version is the reverse of the seamstress' French seam and is used as a simulated welt on the right side of upholstery fabric instead of as an anti-ravel seam finish on the wrong side, as for clothing. (See text, sketch on page 40.)

Gather. To form folds in fabric by drawing it along a drawstring or thread. The folds are left upright.

Gauge. Thickness of material such as sheet metal and wire used in springs.

Gimp. A finishing tape used along exposed wood edges to cover tacks or anywhere a decorative finish is desired. Available in a variety of colors and textures. Double welt is often used in place of gimp tape.

Gimp Tacks. Small tacks designed to hold gimp or to tack invisibly. Their small, rounded heads are barely wider than their shanks.

Glue Block. A piece of wood glued across a joint to reinforce and strengthen it. Also called corner and reinforcing blocks. (See sketch on page 6.)

Glue Injection. A technique for forcing glue into a blind or otherwise inaccessible joint. Drill a $\frac{3}{32}$-inch hole into the joint and use a glue syringe to force in glue until it seeps out the loose joint.

Hinge Link. A U-shaped wire with loops at the wire ends. Used to extend effective length of zig-zag springs, increase spring arc, and soften spring action. (See sketch on page 20.)

Hog Ring. A U-shaped piece of heavy wire with sharply pointed ends which is compressed between the jaws of specially shaped pliers to form a ring.

Low Profile Springs. Any springs which permit the use of seat rails shorter than 3 inches and provide spring action at or barely above rail level, which is not practical with coil compression springs. Zig-zag, rubber webbing, cable, and strap and coil springs are all low profile springs. (See text on page 20, sketches and photos on pages 20, 21, 22.)

Marshall Unit. A group of coil compression springs individually enclosed in fabric pockets and assembled by stitching or hog-ringing together top and bottom coils of adjoining pocketed springs. Sometimes called pocket springs. (See photo on page 19.)

Panel. A stuffed section of cover material used to cover exposed frame, tacks, or bulky pleats, as on the front of round, overstuffed arms. (See text on page 53, sketch on page 54.)

Placket. An opening in fabric, almost always along a seam line, for insertion of closures such as zippers or snaps.

Platform Edge Band. A cover fabric strip stitched with the decking along the back edge of a spring edge roll, then pulled forward over the roll and stitched to the edge wire. (See sketch on page 56.)

Pocket Springs. Any coil compression springs individually enclosed in fabric pockets or cases. (See photo on page 19.)

Pretacked Strips. Tacking strips with tacks inserted every 1 to 1½ inches and tack heads covered by another strip of chipboard or pressed steel strip. Used for blind-tacking leather and synthetic leathers where blind-stitching would be used with covers. (See photo on page 61.)

Pull-through Liner. A wooden slat or strip, added to the frame to provide a tacking point for covers, around which cover fabric is pulled to the outside of the frame. (See sketch on page 7.)

Quilting. The process of stitching in some pattern through cover fabric, a thin layer of stuffing, and a muslin backing. Originally used to make warm clothes and bedding, it is used in upholstery for decorative purposes. (See sketch on page 51.)

Rabbet. A groove cut into a board parallel to the edge, forming a step or ledge. Used to provide a tacking area below exposed wood surfaces to hide raw fabric edges.

Railroad. To run a fabric with its length (warp) parallel to the floor instead of up and down as is normally done. This often is necessary for economy on wide seats and couches. (See sketch on page 47.)

Regulator. A thin, needlelike instrument having either a flattened end or an icepick-style handle. Use to pierce muslin covers and move stuffing underneath. (See text, sketch on page 37.)

Return Arm. Any arm whose stump is set back from the front seat rail.

Return Tie. The portion of a spring-tying twine that has been tacked to the frame and "returned" or brought back up to the topmost coil of the spring next to the rail. (See sketch on page 17.)

Ruching. A pleated ruffle used along the top and sides of frilly boudoir chairs. Simply a smaller version of the pleated skirt, it is sewn into the seam, usually with an accompanying single welt.

Rushing. The process of weaving natural rush or a substitute around the outer edges of a furniture frame to provide a supporting or decorative surface over the frame opening. Also, the woven material. (See text and photos on page 76.)

Self Welt. A length of cord sewn into the fold of a seam allowance to form a ridge. Used the same as a normal welt and where fabric is scarce or too heavy to sew a separate welt into the seam on a home machine. (See text on page 50.)

Shirr. To gather fabric between two drawstrings or between a single draw string and a frame edge.

Show Wood. Any intentionally exposed and finished wood surface on upholstered furniture.

Silencer. Any material used to prevent noise from springs rubbing against supporting surfaces. Usually burlap, rubber, or webbing strips placed between springs and wood frame or support.

Skewer Pins. Large upholsterers' pins used to hold fabrics in place for stitching or measuring. They have loops instead of solid heads.

Skive. To slice at an acute angle to form a taper. Used in joining pieces of leather. (See sketch on page 61.)

Slip-tack. To drive a tack only partway into a surface, usually ⅓ to ½ the tack length, to provide a temporary fastening.

Spline. A strip of wood or rattan, wider at the top than at the bottom, used as a wedge to hold prewoven cane into retaining grooves in slat rails. (See sketch on page 74.)

Spring Edge. The #9-gauge wire (sometimes ¼-inch rattan cane) lashed or clipped to the upper spring coils along exposed edges to provide a firm, unified action to the edge. Also, a descriptive term for construction using this wire edge. (See sketch on page 18.)

Spring-edge Roll. A specific type of stitched edge roll used on spring edges.

Stitched Edge Roll. An edge roll, usually larger than 1½-inch diameter, with one or more rows of stitches which give the roll a triangular cross section shape. (See sketch on page 26.)

Stretcher. A piece of inexpensive fabric attached to the edge of expensive cover fabric to provide a tacking extension where it will be invisible in normal use (sketch, page 51). Also, devices for pulling cushion seams (photo, page 68) and webbing (sketch, page 10) taut.

Tacking Strips. Strips of chipboard ¼ to ½ inch in width, used to reinforce tacked cover edges and edge rolls. Also used in blind-tacking.

Top Padding. Stuffing material used immediately under the covers, usually felted cotton, polyester, kapok, or foam. (See text on page 32.)

Trapunto. A specialized version of quilting used to make a raised, padded pattern on the face of a fabric by stitching through the fabric and a quilt patch on the reverse side. The pattern may be small shapes enclosed in single lines of stitches or a tubular shape enclosed between twin lines of stitches. (See sketch on page 52.)

Tuck-in. Material allowance between seat and arms or seat and back on slip covers, for tucking into the crevice. Tuck-ins give a better appearance and greater durability than a seam sewn at the visible contact point between seat and arms or back.

Tufting. The use of buttons pulled down tightly to the supporting surface to hold the cover and stuffing in place and decorate the surface with raised areas or tufts and sharply defined pleated lines between tufts. (See text, sketch on page 42.)

Undercasing. The fabric cover, usually burlap or muslin, used to enclose coarse fiber stuffing materials where special shapes must be built up, as on arm boards. (See sketch on page 27.)

Venting. The process of providing for the free passage of air into and out of furniture.

Warp. The threads running the length of and parallel to the finished edge of yard goods (the selvage).

Webbing Plier. A gripping and stretching tool with wide, grooved lower jaws, designed to stretch cut webbing and artists' canvases. Also called webbing stretcher.

Weft. The threads carried by the weaving shuttle, across the warp. The threads at right angles to the selvage.

Welt. A cord-filled fabric strip, usually sewn into a seam to protect the seam against wear, emphasize and square off corners, or visually separate cover areas. (See text, photos on page 50.)

Index